AUG 2 '71

P9-DTJ-251

My Stephen Crane

Linson's portrait of Stephen Crane on the threshold of fame.   1894.

CORWIN K. LINSON

MY
STEPHEN
CRANE

Edited with an Introduction
by Edwin H. Cady

SYRACUSE UNIVERSITY PRESS

1958

Library of Congress Catalog Card Number 58-9279

© 1958

SYRACUSE UNIVERSITY PRESS

Contents

List of Illustrations

All these photographs were taken in the 1890's by Corwin Knapp Linson. The annotations on them are in his hand.

Introduction

THROUGH THE CONTINUING GENEROSITY *of Mr. George Arents, the Stephen Crane Collection of Syracuse University has been able to build up holdings of nearly all the known printed items by or about Crane, a small but interesting body of holograph materials, and a number of association items of one sort or another.* One of the collections the University Library was able to acquire in 1953 was that of Crane's friend, the American painter Corwin Knapp Linson. In addition to the letters, bits of manuscript, association pieces, and uniquely valuable photographs in Mr. Linson's collection was the typescript of a volume entitled "Stephen Crane: A Personal Record." This script and its publication rights the University bought from Mr. Linson with the rest of his collection.*

Corwin Knapp Linson has had a distinct and interesting career as an American painter. Born in Brooklyn, New York, in 1864, he grew up there and in Albion, New York, showing his talent as a boy in sketching and making effective copies from the illustrated magazines, like "Harper's Weekly," then popular. Like many of the painters of his time, he got his real professional training in Paris, studying at the Julian Academie, and the École des Beaux Arts, as the pupil of Gérôme, Lafebvre, and Laurens. Gauguin, then equally obscure, was one of Linson's fellows. When he met Stephen Crane in New York in 1891, therefore, Linson was not only seven years older but

* For a representative listing see Appendix III, pp. 75-87, of Cady and Wells, *Stephen Crane's Love Letters to Nellie Crouse* (Syracuse: Syracuse University Press. 1954).

in possession of everything Crane most desired and was most desperately battling to get: professional status, confidence in technique and method, and the economic toehold, however precarious, which enabled him to maintain the studio penniless Steve used for quiet and shelter.

After the period in which Linson associated intimately with Crane, Linson's life was full of interest and variety. "Scribner's" sent him to Athens to sketch the first modern Olympian Games, and the Games authorities awarded him a regular Olympic medal. "McClure's" sent him on Barnum and Bailey's foreign tour to sketch animals. He spent two years drawing in Palestine, mainly to prepare illustrations for John Watson's "Life of Christ." He lived on Mount Vesuvius for a time to record the site and study the volcano's effects on the local inhabitants. He fell in love with Anne G. Prickett, daughter of the United States Consul in Rheims, and was married in Rheims Cathedral.

After Linson's return to the United States with his wife in 1901, he continued to sketch for the "class" magazines. His paintings were exhibited at the Pan-American Exposition of 1901, the St. Louis Exposition of 1904, and at various times at the National Academy of Design, the New York Water Color Club, the Corcoran Gallery, Chicago Art Institute, and Pennsylvania Academy of Fine Arts. He painted landscapes, a number of oil portraits, among them those of Crane, Mark Hopkins, and Edmund Wilson, and did murals and memorial windows for various churches. His works hang in several important galleries.

The manuscript of Linson's recollections of Crane appears to have been written and revised over a period of years during the rebirth of interest in Crane in the early 1920's. It failed of publication then and presumably later, and when it was sold the author had apparently long given up hope of commercial success or even printing for it. It is presented now as a labor of love on the part of editor and publisher— because anything new about Stephen Crane is important, because there is genuine intrinsic interest in Linson's account, and "pour encourager les autres."

Some readers, at least, will want to know what the editor did to Linson's manuscript, and all are entitled to know. One reason why Linson failed to get his book published was that, while his painter's sense carried over beautifully in helping him communicate atmospheres and impressions, it left him devoid of any ordinary notion of narrative structure. He had organized sometimes topically, sometimes chronologically. Only a reader with extraordinary motivation could be expected to follow him. When his observations are reorganized and patterned together into something like properly connected units, their true value becomes more readily available to a reader. There were the usual discrepancies and inconsistencies which had to be checked against one another and resolved if possible. There were certain pages concerned with Linson's career when it did not impinge on Crane's at all, and these pages the editor omitted.

Linson's suave, impressionistic style has been preserved intact to the best of the editor's ability. A few obvious errors or infelicities have been corrected. A minimum of essential connective phrases has been added. Very infrequently what seemed lapses in taste were mended. Twice, for instance, Linson made Stephen Crane say something like, " 'The hair-oil he does!' " That was intolerable, and Crane now says, as surely he really said, " 'The hell he does!' " But on the whole every editorial effort has been exerted to concentrate and clarify Linson's narrative while preserving it as his story, registered through his personality, and speaking his words with his voice.

Every enthusiastic reader of Stephen Crane will find fresh light in this story. The years between Crane's leaving Syracuse University in June, 1891 and the sudden advent of international acclaim for " The Red Badge of Courage" in 1895 have been painfully dark. Really informed, really first-hand views of Crane during those years are almost nonexistent. It now seems probable, in fact, that Linson's is the only such account we shall ever have from within that crowd of medical students and young artists to which Crane belonged. It is worth more than one should attempt to say here to have this view of Crane be a painter's. Much of great worth is recorded about Crane's gentleness, sensitivity, and gallantry, his comradeliness and his integrity, his cockiness—both overt and inverted—his strange, perhaps tragic, awareness of his genius. One finds himself asking fascinating questions. Let us grant that Crane's creative imagination naturally produced visions of man's fate as war. Would that imagination ever have received the germ which produced "The Red Badge of Courage" if Crane had not found it at first comfortable and then fascinating to lie on Linson's studio couch, out of the nasty weather, and read "Century" magazine? Every Craneian will find himself asking comparable questions as a result of Linson's story.

Aside from Corwin Knapp Linson himself, editor and publisher wish to thank Lester G. Wells, Rare Book Librarian and Archivist of the Syracuse University Library, for many valuable suggestions, and Jack Lunn Mowers for indispensable and surprisingly successful assistance in rehabilitating the Linson photographs, some of which have never been published before. We are also very grateful to Mr. Clifton Waller Barrett for his ready generosity in permitting the reproduction of the portrait Linson painted of Crane which is in Mr. Barrett's possession.

EDWIN H. CADY

My Stephen Crane

1

42 West Thirtieth Street: Winter, 1893

THE square hole through which you left the life of the streets was the entrance into a dusty terracotta-tinted hallway, and a stair with a sharp left turn landed you before a door just discernible in the reserved twilight. The building was an ancient, red brick, three-story-and-mansard on the southwest corner of Broadway and Thirtieth Street in the years around 1890. The house has long since gone the way of old New York. In London it might have endured until its decrepit knees sagged and its many eyes grew bleary, but in New York "ancient" becomes a matter of two or three generations. The gray door in that winter of 1893 opened into my studio. What lay in the dim hollows below was of no concern; eighteen dollars monthly rental was my part; and the windows were noncommittal.

Then Stephen Crane developed from the unknown, on a notable afternoon of interminable snow, when the padding whiteness fell as with a persistent purpose to smother the world. The murk of the studio seemed deepened by the crystal blanketing of the outside. Also the industry of casual spiders on the big window was revealed. My affairs harmonizing with the gradually enveloping gloom, steps in the hall and a knock were like the sudden lighting of darkness. Then Stephen Crane entered in the tow of my cousin Louis Senger of Port Jervis.

Crane shed a long rain ulster and was surprisingly reduced in bulk by the process, showing a comparatively slight figure, of medium height, but with the good proportions and poise of an athlete. His face, lean but not thin, was topped by rumpled blondish hair that neither convention nor vanity had yet trained. The barely discernible shading of a mustache had just begun to fringe a mouth that smiled with engaging frankness. Against the window his profile silhouetted in a cleancut reminiscence of the young Napoleon. When later I pointed that out in a March *Century* magazine, he was interested. "But not so hard, Steve," I qualified.

"I hope not," he responded.

It took more than the afternoon's low-keyed light to reveal the quality of his eyes. Something in their gray-blue intensity explained much when later he penned his manuscripts with so precise a phrasing that seldom was a change made in them. But, after all, I had little appreciation that day of his very unusual personality. Had I never seen him again I might some time in the years following have said, "Yes, he came to my den of a place once back in '93, sat on my divan and laughed at Louis' quips and smoked cigarettes, or mostly held them in his fingers until

2

they went out. Those nervous fingers were yellowed with holding dead cigarettes. Between Lou's pipe and Crane's cigarettes I was depleted of matches, just about.

"He didn't talk much. I showed them some pictures and we raved about Sullivan County." But had that been all, this would end right here.

Louis casually introduced him as a friend who wrote things, and me as a cousin who painted things, a common ground of visualizing upon which we accepted one another without further question. But his being a friend who wrote things meant to me only that he was not a bill collector, just then an item much in his favor. There were many writers.

He had a brother living in Port Jervis. My infant reputation in Louis' leading having wandered in that direction, a passing wonder took me. Did this young author want an illustrator? I was "on the job," though they did not say it that way then. There were many illustrators, too. I did not ask, but as the work of writers must come to the illustrators by way of editors, it was our feeling that to editors most illustrators were like tramps scrabbling for handouts. But to the tramps, most editors were pirates. (I came to a better understanding later.) "And most writers are punk," was Crane's notion. His reserve began to crumble. There were a few outstanding exceptions, but most of the magazine stuff was dead, too far gone for funerals. The writers were not artists. "But they get the tin!" Editors again.

Said I, "Reminds me of a day last spring when I went to the art editor of *Leslie's*. I had known him in Philadelphia. He used to have a big studio on Market Street and was so decent to me then that he gave me a drawing of his, even. 'Here's a friend at last,' I thought. Showed him my stuff, and after he'd pawed it over he grunted, 'You can't draw.' That to a man three years with Gérôme and the rest of 'em, and two mentions and a prize at Julian's. Not know how to draw! Say, I was too faint to answer that he never knew what drawing was. I just oozed out of his door

3

like a trickle of water. Now he *had* been a good fellow, but that's what happens to a man when he gets to be an editor."

"Ever try him again?"

"Huh! When I went to study I took my conscience with me. I thought the public wanted honest work, but see the rot it pays its money for! What that editor wanted was photographs."

Happily, times have changed, but when another match went to relight Crane's cigarette, Lou said, "Show us some pictures, CK."*

There was among the lot one that had been painted in the hope of sale as a thread advertisement. But advertisers in those days had little imagination—they have traveled a long way since. A great Jap doll lay prone with a host of tiny dolls tying him to the earth, an excited, curious throng crowding about, balls of thread in odd little carts, and all in a gay flutter of parasols and cherry bloom. Lou suggested a fairy story. "Write something for it, Steve."

Crane studied it solemnly, then presently a wan smile came and went like faint sunshine passing over a shadowy field. "I don't think I could."

Of course it was a trivial doll-Gulliver jest, but children were amused by sillier things and it might have earned a few dollars between us. "No, I couldn't." I was afterward to learn that this boy of twenty† expressed there, without further explanation, a simple ingrained honesty of purpose. He already knew what his art meant to him and could write of life only as he felt it.

Well, put the thing away. We could talk of Port Jervis, where old Point Peter's back humped against the sunsets while he stretched his feet toward the stony bed of the Delaware. Louis says that as between the bald-headed twin peaks of Point Peter and Mount William "nobody knows exactly which is Pete and which is Bill, but it doesn't make much difference except that it

* "Ceek."

† Born November 1, 1871, Crane had recently become 21. (Editor's note.)

4

gives us something to debate about during the long winter months." Old Pete seems almost to hold the village in his lap. They used to call it a "village." As a city it has not grown to the name. It is still a "Whilomville."

Main Street, in its physically elevated distinction, and with no commerce on its entire curving length, overlooks the lower town and its shifting overlay of smoke; a Main Street, as I knew it, without a store, not even a peanut stand. But it may be that at any moment some enterprising son of Hellas may give me the lie and open up under the disapproving frown of old Pete. Near this end of it was the home of Judge Crane,* a broad-porched house faced by spreading lawns. Also among the homes strung along its course was the tiny coop of a house which was to be my summer studio—when I could buy it. It is still there, but not mine.

For Port Jervis boys, the summer, between sleeps, was either time to eat or time to swim. There were occasional diversions in the wilds of the surrounding territory. The town in one direction dawdles out to a valley of some extent with rambling deflections. As croquet gave way to tennis, and tennis side-stepped to golf, a part of this spread of land became extensive links attached to a commodious club house. But the meandering valleys all end in being swallowed by the hills.

The Erie's laboring engines enter from the mountains, and after distributing an incredible volume of smoke impartially over the helpless town, rumble off with their freight into mountains again. They would not be mountains in Colorado, but they are fair for Port Jervis. Another road, diverging from the main tracks, carries several trains daily clanking through the aforesaid valley, when they finally shriek and groan up a heavy grade to the clear serenity of Monticello. These shed their loads of summer boarders all along the way. It was as though they leaked through the windows. Inert baggage used mostly to occupy the regular exits.

On the station platforms were sundry packages, suitcases,

* William Howe Crane.

5

trunks, lunch baskets, and babies. On the trains everyone in shirtsleeves or shirtwaists, when shirtwaists were worn; conductors and passengers in a lather and generously peppered with cinders and smoke-grimed about the ears; infant noses flattened pink about the panes, fans in a flutter, and on the floors a litter of banana skins, peanut shells, and discarded papers. The boys called this road "The Huckleberry Express" because in the season, they said, you "could drop off and feed yourself" with the blue fruit between puffs. (This is as of the 1890's.) And Hartwood is hidden somewhere along the way. This road to Monticello must have been a dismal affair in the winter. In the opening chapter of *The Third Violet*, Crane begins Hawker's life adventure from one of those trains, but at this our first meeting that lovely idyll lay two years in the future.

Finally Louis drew forth a *Cosmopolitan** in which was the story "A Tent in Agony," the scene of which was laid in Sullivan County. That was my county. A country of elastic miles flowing over hills and rocks and around lakes and through hemlock woods and past boarding houses; with stone-walled lanes and stone-bedded trout streams and brooks; sheep pastures, swimmin' holes, and tin peddlers, and snakes, buttermilk and butternuts, chestnuts—alas, no more; huckleberry swamps and blackberry tangles, wild-strawberry shortcakes—but not in the boarding houses; buckwheat cakes a dozen deep—but not in the boarding houses either; buttered hot rye bread with honey; yes, and salt pork and vinegared lettuce with sugar: Sullivan County! This glints and glimmers to those who know from the pages of *The Third Violet*.

But now Crane retired to the darkest end of the divan while I read. His move was natural but needless, for I was caught at once by the deftness of touch and the live humor, and my sympathetic delight spilled over. Then he emerged, and from that moment we were on a rock bottom basis of understanding. We both were like natives of old Sullivan, though neither born there. He told of two

* For December 1892.

6

others, "Four Men in a Cave," and "The Mesmeric Mountain," *
as among the fruits of his and Lou's craving for the wild. A third
in adventure was Fred Lawrence, now long a physician in Philadelphia. Louis said that they once had tried to satisfy their longing
for the gypsy life early one June, and that they "nearly froze to
death." Of their struggle for existence all he recalls is the cold,
and he has never liked winter since.

On comparing data, we found that while Crane was collecting
items (and absorbing "The Pace of Youth" background) around
Asbury Park for his brother Townley in the summer of 1888, the
old Anchor Liner "Alaska" was carrying me to Europe for art
study. Crane was then seventeen, and was to write his first book
before he was twenty. †

But the afternoon was going. "See you again soon," said Crane
on leaving.

"Come and sleep here if you want to, the joint is open house."

---

* For these three and seven other matching pieces, see Schoberlin, ed., *The
Sullivan County Sketches of Stephen Crane* (Syracuse: Syracuse University Press,
1949). (Editor's note.)

† Crane's Asbury Park reporting for the *New York Tribune* had actually been
done in the summer of 1892. (Editor's note.)

7

Crane and Linson on the roof of Linson's studio.

Crane and Linson pose for the lost illustrations for "The Reluctant Voyagers." Crane said, "Gosh! You can brown wheats on this tin!" See page 19.

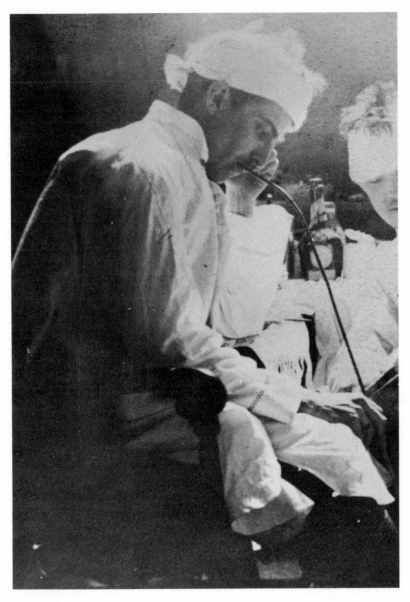

Crane living "The Pace of Youth." Was this the celebration for "Maggie"? See pages 26-28.

Stephen Crane at the Coal Mines
Scranton, 1894 - June

See page 67.

As Linson notes, Crane lay here on his studio couch and read the raw materials for "The Red Badge of Courage" out of the bookcase. See pages 36-37.

2

"Maggie"

IT was a good beginning. Crane's long raincoat became a familiar note in my studio furnishings. In those days of storm it was comfortable to be inside.* Snow and sleet and driving rains, and all the battling of the winter skies could not follow him through the door. Any sense of window clatter or the gale tearing at the cornice would be lost in the creations taking shape upon his pad. It soon became his daily habit to compare the chary dealings

* Verifying the weather of that winter, the records give storms of wind, rain and snow prevailing from mid-November to mid-March.

of our fortunes or to spend hours at a time on a divan.

Another illustrator shared the studio mornings. It meant a mutual economy. He alone made all the drawings used by a certain cheap periodical, and it amused and often irritated Steve to look over the stories brought in by him.

"It seems that my opinions and the opinions of the powers that pay for this stuff are not in agreement. Else I would be asking you out to dinner at the Astor House."

That question of dinner haunted our thoughts, and it was exasperating to see this anemic verbiage and its crude illustrations reap a golden harvest while the art of the since acknowledged master-genius of them all could not find a dependable market. But the quality of brain that accepted the output we saw daily would be unable to distinguish the value of Steve's prose.

Some things we knew because they were so, one of which was that we had to eat. Other things we knew by common report, one of which was that food was to be had at certain resorts of varying cheapness. A wrinkled and yellowed page, dating from that period, whose smoothed creases betray its rescue from an intended oblivion, has survived to witness a state of mind to which Steve was daily subjected for weeks at a time. I think its salvage is justified now; it was but a safety valve to ease the pressure of a mood, and his reputation will not suffer from its printing, while the truth of a certain phase of the Stephen Crane "legend" is amply verified. Near the top is penciled "I'd sell my steps to the grave at ten cents per foot, if 'twere but honestie." Then:

Ah, haggard purse, why ope thy mouth
Like a greedy urchin?
I have nought wherewith to feed thee.
Thy wan cheeks have ne'er been puffed,
Thou knowest not the fill of pride.
Why then gape at me
In fashion of a wronged one?

13

Thou smilest wanly
And reproachest me with thine empty stomach.
Thou knowest I'd sell my steps to the grave
If 'twere but honestie.
Ha! leer not so,
Name me no names of wrongs committed with thee.
No ghost can lay hand on thee and me,
We've been too thin to do sin.
What, liar? When thou wast filled with gold didst I riot?
And give thee no time to eat?
No, thou brown devil, thou art stuffed now with lies as with wealth.
The one gone to let in the other.

Early "lines" which the world never saw, a bit of penny pad wearing the leer of an ironical humor in a lean time.

But this winter and spring was a season of such iron-handed privation for Steve as even I, who saw him at daily intervals, and whose feet were in the same slough, but faintly comprehended. In after years he made his wife shudder at the simple mention of potato salad for breakfast. He told her we just about lived on potato salad for days at a time. I have had time to forget, but it explains a surviving distaste for that useful filler-in for impromptu suppers. It was furnished by a little Sixth Avenue delicatessen shop—it was their cheapest food—and I have shied at delicatessens ever since. It once was considered the inestimable privilege of painters and poets to live in attics and for dinner to roast chestnuts over a candle flame. It added forty-eight per cent to the romance of biographies. Now I have been caught that way, and the romance is minus. (I even wonder now how I came by the chestnuts.) But I believe that the theory once rejoiced in, that inspiration thrived on emptiness, has been smashed.

Steve sedulously hid his need from his own kin. And, while he occasionally borrowed—when I had it—a quarter from me, he never named any possible use for it. The days must have worn a face of stone. If you are hungry it is because you have no family. If you have no family you are an outcast. If you are an outcast you deserve to be hungry. This is not given as personal conviction, but as the world's logic. Steve put it thus in *The Third Violet*: "Poverty! . . . Poverty is everything to be ashamed of. A fellow isn't a man and doesn't stand up straight unless he has some money."

No, his family did not know. His own people thought the later stories of hardship were told only to give the color of romance to the tales. They could not understand how they could be true, with their own homes so gladly open to him at his option. Well, I happen to know.

One does make light of it afterward, but at the time: "Singular thing," he wrote, "you get so frightfully hungry as soon as you learn that there are no more meals in sight!" That was no academic reflection. It was born of bitter experience.

And it is humiliating to have to own that the work of your brain and hand is not even feeding you. That was at bottom the reason of Steve's reticence with his friends. How one hated to go to relatives in the city with anything like the appearance of wanting a dinner! It is undoubtedly difficult to be a dignified beggar.

I was then making drawings at four dollars each, and little details like a quarter or a half-dollar passing from my pocket to Steve's gaping purse were unnoted until one day it transpired that there were no pennies in the bank. Steve, after a morning's work, was just leaving, his foot on the stair. I hesitated, then in desperation I called through the door, "Hey! Steve! If you have fifty cents we'll eat together." Impecunious Steve halted, then an apologetic voice said, "Not a red, CK." Instantly sorry that I had asked, I said so, and he passed on, smiling grimly. I have happily forgotten how I fared that day, nor did I ever know what comfort Steve had.

He had loyal friends, but while some had more than others, no one ever quite overflowed. And one or two were always on the near side of enough. There were young medics in hospital work, cub reporters, Louis who came down from Port Jervis when he had the price, and others here and there. When an unexpected freak of fortune brought oysters and beefsteak within reach, there was a celebration. Joyous times! And yet turkey was then but thirteen cents a pound; but to be available it had to be cooked. We had no kitchen. Of the cheap ready-cooked cereals of today we had not one.

An eating place called "The Boeuf-a-la-mode" was typical of that certain New York life of the early nineties. It was an unsavory resort on Sixth Avenue which we promptly rechristened "The Buffalo Mud." It was a place to wallow in. We foregathered at this cook-shop on Saturday evenings because only then could the various "Indians" be assembled. A second reason was that it was scandalously cheap, and, third, it possessed the allurement of the unexpected. It was never known what the unforeseen might bring forth; anything was permitted that would not bring the police.

We always surrounded a central table. In case of a riot it was handy to the exit. The guests "dined noisily and with great fire, discussing momentous problems furiously, making wide maniacal gestures through the cigarette smoke. . . . The little handful of waiters ran to and fro wildly . . . they struck two blows at a table and left there a knife and fork . . . the clatter of this business was wild and bewildering." So wrote Steve in *The Third Violet*. As these eating aids were conjured from cavernous pockets, we bestowed further attention carefully with our napkins, these and the cloths often liberally stained with spilled wine or the legitimate uses of previous diners. Then our handkerchiefs were better. "The Buffalo Mud" practiced much economy as to laundries.

Each diner about us seemed immensely pleased with himself. The gas lights flickered in the drafts, and the smoke lazily eddied overhead or was suddenly shattered before a blast from "A Hot Time in the Old Town Tonight," sung to a beating of spoons on the bottles and glasses not in the least disconcerting to any neighbor intent on playing his own tune. It was like the practice hour of a Turkish band.

If we enjoyed that once, to cite Crane's Hawker, we "don't like it so much any more. . . . A man would be a fool if he did like this dinner." However, we never pretended to. It was what went with the dinner that appealed, and for differing reasons. As illustrators or writers we each got a certain material. Crane found there pages for his *Third Violet*, and possibly passages that colored other work as yet unthought of, for even *The Third Violet* lay in the mists of a year thence. The artist never knows when or how life will present itself for his use; for months or years the matter lies dormant, then suddenly the thing is at his fingers' ends. So let it come to him as it might. Steve knew it was there. Art will not be hunted.

So we left our napkins to the next comers.

Later stories had it that Stephen Crane was often given to common speech about women. I aver that in all his talk throughout the years I never heard a cheap jest from his lips. Always unreserved with his intimates, he once expressed admiration for a small vaudeville twinkle of red—he was fond of red—and a saucy soprano warble, and had it echo back with unsavory additions. His scorn was vocal.

"Whoever said that can put his nose in some more dirt! She's only a nice little kid doing singing stunts because she has to eat."

There clings to memory one evening call with Steve somewhere uptown. Name and place are gone. We entered a long high-ceiled room, with two deep windows topped with competent lambrequins from which hung lacy drapes looped in state over a heavy curtaining harnessed to the trim. The purpose of windows being to see out of and to breathe in from, all this pomp quite defeated both uses. Added shades of green and white completed this defeat and shut out the universe.

But within was a soft splendor from a mass of dangling prisms, under which sat our young hostess. I remember an uneasy distrust of that gorgeous scintillation suspended over her, as I sat in a window embrasure under the downward sweep of drapery. I felt like a portrait looking out from a wall, and was almost as silent. Here was a young author to question, and there followed a rapid fire of debate:

Were not women justified on public platforms?

"No!"—he had his memories.

Why were "purpose novels"? But they weren't!

"But you—"

"Oh, I know what you would say, but you can't find preaching on any page of *Maggie*! An artist has no business to preach."

"Then you can't have—"

"Why certainly! A story must have a reason, but art is—oh, well, not a pulpit. Ask CK."

But as I was not known to the girl by that intimate abbreviation she only smiled at me and said it wasn't necessary, she knew what he meant.

"Well then, why—"

It was her turn. "Oh, I just wanted to hear you say it."

When we were again on the street, the chatter and gay laughter becoming a part of an eternity of yesterdays, Steve said nothing for two or three blocks. Then all at once he turned. "CK! Didn't you like it? I don't know anything finer than the natural talk of a nice girl with brains in her head."

No statement of mood is final, and there were many words while all the walk back we discussed the evening. It had been refreshing, delightfully revealing. Only for a little had they referred to his work, their talk searching the avenues of young interests.

I was the portrait, listening from the wall.

The winter was a memory and we were in late spring when Steve brought in a manuscript asking if I cared to make pictures for it. Two men, bathing, had rested and dozed on a derelict raft, and while "lapping waves sang little rippling sea-songs about them," had been carried out to sea. "Night finally settled . . . and a moon came and looked at them." Then a sea-captain found them, so he was important.

Prospecting down the water front, we wandered along the docks, hoping the master of a small coaster would be loafing on the wharves. But while we saw longshoremen and all the business of sea-goers, no sea-captains were visible, and but one small schooner with two of the hands idling on the fore deck. Steve regarded them hopelessly.

"The jays must be doing the Bowery. Anyway, these other bucks are ocean kings. Too high-toned for us. Just make him like a Sullivan County farmer with chin whiskers!"

Which is what I eventually did. A block back from the river the day was stewing with heat. "Let's have an ice cream, Steve."

"Get one for yourself, CK, but I don't like ice cream." What? That was a new one! And in the days when you could have a plate full for ten cents. Well, I could do without too.

In the studio, my roof ladder became the one down which the captain—with chin whiskers—"brought a coffee pot from the sky." Out of the expanse of red tin roof under the full sun Steve and I were snapped for the two men on the beach. "Hurry up there!" he shouted to the camera. "Gosh! You can brown wheats on this tin!" And for once he swore that absolute truth was not essential to a work of art.

As far as I was concerned, the history of "The Reluctant Voyagers" was unfortunate. Landed, a bulky package, in the office of a responsible magazine, it went into retirement and we waited. One has always to do a full amount of waiting.

For me, six months were spent in the wilds of Ramapo, while Steve put in a shorter time at his brother Edmund's. The story for some minor change was returned to Steve. On resubmission, the privilege of a responsible magazine was used to promptly lose all trace of my packet of drawings. They disappeared as it were from the earth, a total loss to me. He is deserving of a niche in the Hall of Fame who can explain how such things come to pass.

At the time of a similar but much later experience, a small daughter sensed the load of disaster and proposed punishment. "Oh! that MEAN old editor! I'll tell you what let's do! We'll go up there, and sister will hold his head down, and I will hold his legs, and you can SPANK him!" That eight-year-old effervescence blew harmlessly into the air. The editor never knew what he missed.

But it was not so bad for Stephen. "The Reluctant Voyagers" survives in several printings.

One morning Steve entered the studio with a sagging pocket. He finally turned out a thin paper-covered book, handing it to me. "Read it, CK, when I leave. May I do some writing?" I glanced at the book. It was a scant half-inch thick, saffron hued, red-lined at top and bottom, with MAGGIE in heavy black between. Its author's name, "Johnston Smith," meant nothing—I knew no Johnston Smith. But the divan had absorbed Steve, rings of smoke circling about him, so I deferred questioning. With pad on his knee, he wrote steadily on.

It was by now a regular thing. Several of the short tales that are a part of his permanent achievement he wrote there in that corner, with a marvelous facility for finishing a story in a morning, or partly developing an idea to lay it aside. That afternoon I took up the book.

My unasked question of the morning, "Why should Steve be interested in any Johnston Smith?" was answered on the first page. It was Steve himself, of course. No other wrote like that, or would begin a tale with anything like the stride of this one. And no writer but Steve would make a mother to stir up a room "until her children were bobbing about like bubbles." His distinctive individuality was in every line. Reading about these people was quite as unpleasant as living with them would be, except for the enjoyment of his art. In fact I did not feel at times that I was reading about them, but that I was with them.

The next morning when I asked for the book, Steve said with a smile, "There are heaps of them left. The public isn't crazy about having 'em." No, it seemed determined not to touch the book. It was "brutal, coarse, cruel"; the public's eye saw only what it called "its vulgar realism." It expected Rum Alley to be written of in terms of upper Fifth Avenue, or to be ignored entirely. "Why write of such people at all?" But that questions the inherent freedom of choice of the artist. Obeying the public, or a hard necessity, he is ground between millstones—or is no artist. In either case he achieves nothing. The artist is the paradox that must do what he is born to do, yet must make his own choice if his work is to live.

"But Steve, why Johnston Smith? Why not your own name? Huh! Johnston Smith!"

That smile, half savage, half amused, wholly sardonic, returned. "They said I might be arrested!" He grinned broadly now. Arrest of course was a joke. But he told me things. *Maggie* was a survival of a tacit boycott declared upon it in 1891. The printing had been his own affair, but he did not say how the cost had been met. The alias was a mere chance. "Commonest name I could think of. I had an editor friend named Johnson,* and put in the 't,' and no one could find me in the mob of Smiths. But no one would sell it, not even the jays who otherwise would sell their souls for a nickel. I sent copies to some preachers who were maniacs for reform—not a word from one of 'em.

"I wrote across the cover so they couldn't miss it, that if they read it, they would see its sense. I knew they'd jump at first, but I hoped they were intelligent. You'd think the book came straight from hell and they smelled the smoke. Not one of them gave me a word! Icebergs, CK, flints!"

* Willis Fletcher Johnson, then day editor of the *New York Tribune*.

The war of the dealers was simple stupidity, which he scorned, but this slight put upon his frankly avowed intention galled him. His integrity had been questioned. If the book was seen to be gross, that beam was in the eye of his critics. The clear-visioned Howells said that *Maggie* had the quality of a Greek tragedy. "As a study of New York life *Maggie* is a remarkable book. There is much realism of a certain kind in it that unfits it for general reading, but once in a way it will do to tell the truth as completely as *Maggie* does."* It was precisely the brutal cruelty of life as it touched little Maggie that Crane wanted to expose to view.

Can the final judgment whether that life can be written of at all be left with a shallow reading public? Steve later put his own opinion into *The Third Violet*. "Oglethorpe contended that the men who made the most money from books were the best authors. Hollanden contended that they were the worst. Oglethorpe said that such a question should be left to the people. Hollanden said that the people habitually made wrong decisions on questions that were left to them." As Hollanden reflects Crane to some extent, we have here the grist of a finely ground conviction. "The voice of the people"—? No! Experience has taught that it habitually makes wrong decisions!

Maggie was written from the heart of a boy who was a bit over nineteen when he showed the manuscript to Willis Fletcher Johnson in the summer of 1891. "Asked me to read it and tell him what to do with it. . . . It was in some respects crude, but powerful and impressive. Three features were conspicuous . . . mastery of the speech and manners of the slums . . . the throbbing vitality and dynamics of the story . . . and despite the astounding frankness of it, the absolute lack . . . of the 'sex-motive' which now-a-days dominates so much of our fiction."†

Against its background of wretchedness is drawn young Jimmie

* *New York Press*, April 15, 1894.
† "The Launching of Stephen Crane," *Literary Digest International Book Review*, April, 1926. [See Vol. IV, 288-90.]

of the chronic sneer, who "menaced mankind at the intersections of streets" and grew up to be a truck driver whose only god was a fire engine, yet could be impressed—within his limitations—with the calm beauty of a full moon. His little sister Maggie "blossomed in a mud-puddle. . . . None of the dirt of Rum Alley seemed to be in her veins." As she grew, "her dim thoughts were often searching for far away lands where the little hills sing together in the morning. Under the trees of her dream-gardens there had always walked a lover."

It almost makes one jump to come upon a like bit of poetry in the course of sordid fact, but that is one charm of Stephen's prose. Yet having allowed himself that small liberty, he thereafter holds himself to the inevitable sequence of events, and makes no appeal they themselves do not evoke. The pathetic figure of Maggie is the more pathetic because she is left entirely in the reader's hands, and such restraint in a writer of nineteen is nothing short of genius.

James Henry Moser, an artist friend of Steve's, wrote to Frederick G. Gordon* on November 16, 1894, "*Maggie* is called fragmentary—that a work to challenge the books that be must have ample leaves. I insist that they are wrong. Prune almost any of the great works to *Maggie*'s dimensions and where are they? Maggie is masterful in technique—its freedom from cheap moralizing makes its lesson all the more vivid; . . . Thank Stephen again for me."

Moser died in 1913, Fred Gordon in 1925. Thinking back about that group of struggling talents, one feels the pressure of the unavoidable changes of the years. We continually expect to go our ways, to say farewell and resume touch and speech as we please. But the reminders are constant that such expectations are futile. Moser, Gordon, Vosburg, Green, all of whom I casually parted with in the nineties, and never saw again; and others even gone as names from memory, yet of earth or not of earth, all once

* One of the Twenty-third Street group, and designer of the cover for *The Black Riders*.

23

tingling with ambitions and very much alive, exist no more for me except in thought.

The memory of two years of a boyhood under ten spent in certain outskirts of Brooklyn gave me an appreciation of those first sentences of *Maggie*, where "A very little boy stood upon a heap of gravel for the honor of Rum Alley. He was throwing stones at howling urchins from Devil's Row who were circling madly about the heap and pelting him." On the borders of Greenpoint were outlying meadows and a sluggish stream called Newtown Creek. Periodically there surged from this placid district a band of young vandals swarming like suddenly released hornets, yelling and swaggering up the slopes armed with clubs, sticks, stones, or whatever ammunition the streets and gutters afforded. To all of us smaller and law-abiding citizens it was the invasion of Huns. Terror flew before their progress and lingered behind their going.

As the word was passed, "Here come the Dangertowners! Here they come! Dangertowners!" we would hear the challenging rattle of sticks on palings and the crash of brickbats into front yards, and from behind the shelter of windows would watch the roaring gang sweep by. They were in truth but a lot of big boys, but to us they were devouring giants. Sometimes suddenly in a vacant lot, a pelting of stones would descend and lead to hand-to-hand battle; and the melee would rage until the uproar would get behind various overlooking windows and our bleeding warriors would be gathered in for much needed repairs.

My brother was once thrown bodily into a bonfire and severely burned; snowballs would be water-soaked and frozen over night, and life-long scars still witness to the ferocity of these attacks. There might or might not have been a policeman in the next ward. How many of these young bullies, I wonder, afterward became aldermen and grew fat on the development of that real estate?

3

"The Pace of Youth":
Spring, 1893

STEVE was in the studio one morning when Emile Stangé, a painter friend from New Jersey, opened my door. He thought Crane a good-looking blond boy with almost nothing to say. But Steve's habit of reticence in the presence of strangers was deceptive. It was as misleading in its way as his apparently idle lounging was in another. One later day he was lying at full length on the divan smoking, entirely oblivious of Stangé pawing over my summer canvases—this was in November of '93. A word shot into the air about the luxury of laziness. Instantly through the smoke waves came the retort, "I'm probably working a great deal harder just now than either of you!"

Now this is jumping over a whole summer. It was in the spring-time that their first meeting took place, when Stangé learned that Crane was a young writer under the ban of the newsdealers who dreaded visits from the agents of Anthony Comstock. Di-rectly, Comstock could not have been at all concerned. Evildoers of a certain type hid like rats in their holes when he was named, but he was not after such as Steve. Remotely, however, consider-ing the panic of the newsstands, the result was the same. Law, abstractly, is but a matter of so many words, but embodied in a personality is to be reckoned with. The condition which Mr. Howells found so hard to understand—and the rest of us with him—may after all have been very simple. Crane's work at no time could fall under Comstock's ban, but the newsstand has no vision. It was unfortunate, certainly, that Steve's white intention should have been seen through sulphured glasses. The irony of that situation glitters in the light of present-day license.

One day I was told that I was expected at a "pow-wow" to be held in Steve's rooms on Avenue A* near East Fifty-seventh Street. A good dozen young fellows were in happy accord with each other and a corpulent punch bowl to which each new arrival was conducted with extravagant ceremony. Besides this wassail bowl, the only other feature of the rooms to be remarked was the lack of chairs and a profusion of mustard-color paper-covered books knee-deep along the wall under the table upholding the punch. It developed that all these little volumes of one color were also of one title, duplicates of my copy of *Maggie*. There were more *Maggie*'s there than I had inclination to count. The party was a sort of birthday anniversary of their printing, and I made mental calculation at the printed price of fifty cents of sales run-ning into hundreds of dollars. Certainly New York would stand in line for a book to be had for fifty cents, for each guest on being

* 1064 Avenue A, rooms shared with Fred Lawrence, October 1892 to May 1893.

presented with a copy hailed it with delight. I could have had an armful but for my qualms about robbing a poor author.

What of today's booksellers and that freight of yellow volumes? If Brentano's once accepted a dozen of them and returned ten, what of having them now for the "privately printed" first edition market? "Can't get in enough Stephen Crane items," once wrote Meredith Janvier to me from Baltimore. But where are they now, those hundreds left with his friend Mrs. Armstrong—who once had the privilege of spanking him—and all those he had with him in his various lodging places? Surely what Thomas Beer relates of Jennie Cregan's use of the books for the kitchen stove surpasses all records for expensive kindling. As to our party, after the first introduction the books rested undisturbed except when used as a seat.

Crane later "discovered the great truth that when one submits himself to a thoroughly conventional conversation he runs risks of being most amazingly stupid." We were not running that hazard now, with the resources of fertile minds trained to many inventions. Steve was ever fond of the hum and twang of a guitar. He began thrumming chords, and soon the "Indians" were chanting to the rhythmic pound of a war dance. It was near midnight when from below came a warm protest: "One couldn't sleep down stairs; one rented rooms to gentlemen, not animals." The sarcasm caught Steve's fancy. He called through the door while waving a frantic hand behind, compelling quiet, "The animals apologize and will return to their cages at once!" And to us, "Cheese it!" We did. After all, we were not rowdies, just youthfully forgetful of the world. I think that even the abused landlady had forgotten us within the week.

As Fifty-seventh Street and Avenue A is some distance from Broadway at Thirtieth, at least two of the animals had a long trail to their cage. And under the circumstances, it was to them a great benefit.

It was not long after this that I again made the trip to these rooms, this time in the early morning. My knock at his door was answered by a short, "Come in!" By a far window sat Stephen, with a towel turban-like about his head. An ink bottle was on a chair beside him, sheets of foolscap on his knees, and with no further ceremony he continued his work. Presently pages were tossed to me, "The Pace of Youth" written at the top of one. Certain "indomitable whiskers" caught my eye, then a "young tarrier" and a girl named Lizzie, and I was lost. Steve had nearly finished, and when I stopped he handed me more and stretched wearily back. I read on to the end. "Like it?" he asked laconically. Of course I liked it. That girl in a red dress—it would be red!—"crawling slowly like some kind of spider on the fabric of nature"—Stimson going out to smoke and revel in himself—the symbolism of the old horse that became "intent upon his aged legs and spread them in quaint and ridiculous devices for speed" pursuing "the eager spirit of a young and modern horse"—the little glass eye of derision in the rear of the elopers' buggy. That vehicle was "youth, with youth's pace; it was swift flying with the hope of dreams." Of course it escaped, as youth eludes age; Stimson was defied by the derisive eye, by the universe; he suddenly became conscious that his bald head was hatless.* Well, he was not responsible for the smiles that were "soft and prayerful caresses," nor for the careening gay paper lanterns that "sang a chorus of red and violet and green and gold; a song of the mystic bands of the future." Not responsible for any of it but that one little sign, "Cashier," which, "hanging upon the silvered netting behind which the girl sold tickets got directly in range and interfered with the tender message." Responsible only for interference, and that was as impotent as age itself.

"How do you feel all these people so long after you've seen them? It's months since you were down there." He smiled. "Can't you make sketches from memory? Of course. Well, haven't I known these types since I was a kid? Certainly." That was it. And so beautifully felt: color emotion like a painter's, the purple ex-

* In a world where hats were as essential as shoes.

panse of ocean, ghostly sea-froth in an envelope of blue mystery; and how deftly that bit of prose poetry is saved from the sentimental by the comic contrast of people unable in the wind to hear the music but reassured by seeing "the band with their lips glued to their instruments."

"A bird of a story, Steve!"

He warmed to my appreciation, while through his cigarette smoke I studied his headgear. "Yeh! the towel? This thing got me going and I couldn't sleep, so I got up. Been at it all night. A wet towel cools the machinery all right. And I work better at night. I'm all alone in the world. It's great!"

"The Pace of Youth" appears, unabridged, as I read it that morning in New York, in Heinemann's English edition of *The Open Boat*, 1898.

I would pass over some of this time as of little consequence, which it all may be, but that it reveals the early Stephen (though he scarcely lived to be anything else). No opinion is as unalterable as granite, and his he changed frequently, but in his attitude toward his work he never swerved. This attitude is fully expressed in his letter to John W. Hilliard, at that time an editor in Rochester, New York, and one of his early friends.

The one thing that deeply pleases me is the fact that men of sense invariably believe me to be sincere. I know that my work does not amount to a string of dried beans—I always calmly admit it—but I also know that I do the best that is in me without regard to praise or blame. When I was the mark of every humorist in the country, I went ahead; and now when I am the mark for only fifty percent of the humorists of the country, I go ahead; for I understand that a man is born into the world with his own pair of eyes, and he is not at all responsible for his vision—he is merely responsible for his quality of personal honesty. To keep close to this personal honesty is my supreme ambition.*

* From Vincent Starrett's "Stephen Crane, An Estimate," in *Men, Women and Boats*, Boni and Liveright, 1921. Quoted in part by Thomas Beer in *Stephen Crane*.

29

The first comment on his art that I heard from Stephen was that a story should be logical in its action and faithful to character. Truth to life itself was the only test, the greatest artists were the simplest, and simple because they were true. Usually it takes some time for youth to find this out, but Steve knew it by intuition, and also intuitive was his feeling for the unusual approach. His was not a studied technique, he was not self-conscious about it, it was to him simply the way an artist should sense his work. He may in later years have acquired an appreciation of himself, but at no time was there any conceit, only an innate certainty of power. He possessed genius, and knew it, and that was all there was to it. And his intimates knew it too; they rejoiced in it and were glad to be his friends. If others rankled because their little talents paled beside his, they became his enemies.

I was often entertained beyond measure by his outbursts of wrath at the commonplace narrative with its obvious sentimental appeal. Some trivial remark lit the fireworks. "That's TRIPE, CK!" he flashed at me.

"True, at any rate," I shot back. And there I delivered myself to the block forthwith.

"True? Of course it's true, as all platitudes are true! But they're tiresome, tiresome as mud."

One day he was reading in his usual corner when suddenly the magazine hurtled to the floor. "Any writer who will use such a mildewed phrase as 'from time immemorial' ought to have his brain sluiced! These mutts," he traced sundry curves in the air with my long churchwarden, "who write with a phrase dictionary in their eye should be digging sewers. Their English is cast iron. . . . There goes your pipe, CK! Sorry, old man, you shouldn't have these antiques on your shelves." The long stem, not being cast iron, had snapped into fragments.

That pipe figures in a curious photograph. I was leveling my camera at Steve as he sat against a Japanese rug—from Macy's, Macy's of Fourteenth Street—and thought him quietly puffing the long clay. When developed, the plate showed fountain jets of pipe stems and several vaguely suggested hands, and a barely discernible face. "Call it a portrait of Steve Crane in animated conversation," was his laughing comment.

Steve reveled in the use of words as a painter loves his color. To create unusual images with them, odd conceits, quaint similes, was as natural as to eat when meal time came. He loved to cut his phrases sharply.

His passion for realism was tinctured all through by the glow of imagination in even his simplest tales. And this passion accounted for his respect for the crystal sincerity of Howells and Garland. He never mentioned their style. In that period, "style" came near to being worshiped as the end of art, as the only thing worth while; but Steve cared little how a man worked—a simple fidelity to a man's own vision held his loyalty. His art—of course he must be an artist—could take care of the rest.

He had no use for the old school of romance novelists. There was plenty of true romance in ordinary life. He would have agreed with Mark Twain about Scott, but for other reasons put the screws on Mark. "This whoop over his stuff contaminates the air."

"Now, Steve, you don't mean all that. Of course, anybody can shoot holes in anybody. Mark's all right."

"I didn't say HIM, I said his *stuff*. Sam Clemens is all right, but Mark Twain—" Well, he did not quite mean all of that either, for where Mark wrote of real life in his *Mississippi* book, even Mark was "all right."

A smile comes with the remembrance of the two youths in their twenties discussing the giants, among them Victor Hugo. It was enough for Steve if even the shadow of a pose fell across the page. He argued that self-conscious work was bad as art. I agreed. "Of course it is, or it isn't art at all. Who said it wasn't bad?"

"Well, then—?"

"No, Steve, I didn't say—"

"But you *were* saying—"

"No, I'm only *trying* to say that in Hugo I come across fine situations, and I pass by the bare canvas for the big pictures. Then, too, he carries me away by the very weight of his impetus. Some of his sentences weigh tons."

"But that's just words, CK. He pulls on the scales. I can always see him peering out to see how he hits you." Steve did spoil some illusions. But we enjoyed it—and I still enjoy Hugo, at times, even if he does peer at me.

Parrying with nonsense in tight places was diverting. Walking down Sixth Avenue one day we passed a stand placarded "Hot Tamales." Steve had not yet been in Mexico, but he talked of tamales as one to whom they were like bread. So I asked him what they were like. "Don't you know what tamales are?"

I shriveled in my ignorance. "No, I don't. What are they like?"

"You don't know what tamales are? You're a bird!"

"Maybe, but you're a highflyer yourself. What are they?" Then a side glance showed him laughing. "Ha! I don't believe you know yourself."

"You implacable Indian, to corner me that way. Of course I don't."

This time I came out whole, but Senger and Crane occasionally left me on the stretcher.

There hung on my wall a small painting of cows in a wintry barnyard around a central haybox. "Now that sketch, CK. That's the real thing." Then with eyes and a finger he made a silently eloquent gesture of request. "Well, some day, Steve, when you have a place for it." I thought that safe, and he never did come into its actual possession, though he stole it in his own way and put it in *The Third Violet*. In his subconsciousness there may even then have been gathering some gossamer threads of the tale.

He had a way of noting random sentences on paper scraps long before he would find their fitting places. On such I find: "A ghastly, ineffaceable smile sculptored by fingers of scorn," the "*o*" as written. "A fierce little stove." "Littered with straw, tin cans and children." "The door clanged behind him." "In a large vaulted hall that blazed with light." Doubtless most of these waifs were adopted sooner or later, but of the ever-increasing family of them born of his thought many must have dropped by the way. He would never miss them, they sprouted like seed under showers. They are instances of a haphazard inspiration before it crystallizes into purpose.

Stephen always welcomed sympathetic criticism and valued it from competent minds. He told me one day with great satisfaction that John D. Barry of the *Forum* had given him valuable counsel, suggesting more talk between his characters because "talk reveals, it lightens narrative," and had also written a six-page letter of friendly criticism of *Maggie*, a letter which touched Steve for its proof of genuine interest.

Steve did not care for Dickens nor have much use for any of the older school or tradition. Crane's was peculiarly the genius for distilling from a given situation its very essence, fixing it on the page in swift impressionistic sentences tingling at times with a perfect expression, always alive. His longest tales to 1898 were not really novels but long short-stories turning on incidents occupying but little time. Now those whose idea of a novel is an involved plot and analysis, and a fabric built up with the constructive solidity of a skyscraper, meet here with a writer whose pages are put together with a magic of words built around an episode, words used with the skill of a conjurer who seldom slips, whose paragraphs flash with the unexpected and whose sentences charm with the quaint definition, the simile supremely fit, like a shot to the bull's-eye.

He would laugh to himself as he wrote, and I knew that there was joy in store for a future responsive reader. If Steve disliked Dickens' overstressed appeal, it was a question of a difference in art standards. Dickens was an amazing magician, or he was a caricaturist, not ever a realist. Stephen felt that he always had his eye on his audience. Le Gallienne might have said of Crane what he did say of another: "His concern was with the faithful presentation of character and story . . . with no intrusion whatever of the writer's personality." And the last clause is the key to Stephen's whole attitude toward writing: an author should keep himself out of his story and his characters in; "the public doesn't care a rip about the author's opinions." His genius was that which took the reader at once into his situations, enabling him as an immediate spectator to see what was going on.

The scrupulous sincerity which drew Conrad and Crane together was in Steve's case carried to the limit when he refused to elaborate parts of *The Third Violet* for their betterment because the story had already appeared in print. One would suppose that an artist had the privilege of improving his work for the benefit of his next audience, if not for his own sake.

He had just been reading Olive Schreiner's *Story of an African Farm:* "She is a woman of sense and an artist," he said with warmth. He had no liking for the somber moods of Ambrose Bierce, and Stevenson he would not read. "Not *Treasure Island?*"

"Well, yes, a good story for kids." He just could not take the sunny R. L. S. seriously.

As I pause in memory of those days I see a pair of serene blue eyes and a quiet smile that lights the whole of a face that otherwise appears dimly. The sound of his voice comes to me, and the quick turn of the body, but it is the smile that lingers.

4

Genesis of
"The Red Badge of Courage":
1893

$\mathbb{F}$ROM my studio all through the week could be heard the intense activity of Broadway. For some time I wondered why it was that so often there should be such a frenzy of gongs and clatter of hoof and wheel until I discovered that I dwelt over a route most frequented by the fire engines then drawn by horsepower. And just around the corner near Twenty-ninth Street was Daly's theater, the cause of nightly riot of megaphones roaring for vehicles which seldom responded in the order called. Also the din of clacking hoofs, wheels grinding against curbs or colliding with other wheels, raucous ironies of disputing cabbies, and the chatter and laughter and shuffling of countless feet from the sidewalks; and still the howling of the megaphones. I then sensed what Crane afterward wrote: "New York roars always like ten thousand devils." But in a little time the roar became like the buzzing of flies in my sleep, and I was awakened only in times of sudden hush.

Every day the noise began like the first notes in a frog pond. An echo of heels in an increasing patter, a jangle of horse cars— they soon put in cables—milk cans banged to a restaurant door— cans and a dipper then!—then suddenly all the business of the city yawped along outside until the climax of the megaphones. At that corner New York dozed between twelve and four in the morning.

They played Shakespeare joyously in that theater. From a small alcove I could climb a convenient ladder to the flat roof, where errant air currents brought such enticing echoes that once I was led to forego a dinner that in the delightful company of Ada Rehan, George Clarke, and James Lewis I might forget that New York exacted blood-money for food and rents. Today, Shakespeare is little more than a name on a book.

But another book that was to be oftener on the world's tongue than Shakespeare in the middle nineties was in embryo then. In Stephen Crane's consciousness there was a seed-thought taking root and coming to growth. He was immersed in dreams.

It was at this period that his hopes of even a sufficiency met with temporary defeat. He had said, "If I had a new suit of clothes I'd feel my grip tighten on the future—it's ridiculous but it doesn't make me laugh." A year later *The Red Badge* blazed in the columns of the syndicate press, and then for a time faded.

In my studio the divan he mostly inhabited was on one side of the big window. On the other side was an oaken bookcase. Old magazines met me on my walks and made love to me, flew at me from bookstalls, and rode me home. And so this case was

36

stacked with *Century*'s containing *The Battles and Leaders of the Civil War*. Justly proud of these records of American valor, their writers were particularly careful to narrate with an exactness that omitted no detail of just what took place in every action. Here was the wooded knoll, there rode the generals, elsewhere the formation of troops; one regiment did this, the enemy did something else, such a result from a battle, but nothing that might by any chance be outside of historic fact, or give the personal reaction. What *happened* was told down to the last belt and button. After all, as history it was the best possible because it was written by the participants; but curiously enough this vast amount and precision of detailed information was just what made Steve recoil. He was squatting like an Indian among the magazines when he gave one a toss of exhausted patience and stood up.

"I wonder that *some* of these fellows don't tell how they *felt* in those scraps! They spout eternally of what they *did*, but they are as emotionless as rocks!"

This happened to be the one remark from Steve during the whole of the time he was thus engaged.

Just here, by way of contrast, is as beautiful a bit as Steve ever wrote. In its charm of suggestion it is unsurpassed:

"When the snow fell upon the clashing life of the city, the exiled stones, beaten by myriads of strange feet, were told of the dark silent forests where the flakes swept through the hemlocks and swished softly against the boulders." *

And that was what we looked out upon while he was so concerned with the quality of dullness of the Civil War records.

Stangé had given me a small sketch of a great white cruiser at anchor in the North River against the line of city towers. Steve at once entitled it, "The Sense of a City Is War." "Clashing life," struggle, change, exile. The very pavements were not at home.†

* *The Third Violet.*

† Cobbles and paving stones, no motors to demand asphalt or cement. It seems now incredible that Steve never saw an automobile in New York.

Snowflakes were trampled by the city's throngs while Steve thumbed over the magazines, searching for the thing that eluded him, to leave them in disorder on the floor. But one day he said, "I'm through with 'em now, CK. Your charming patience is appreciated!" But I do not recall that he replaced them!

He seemed one urged by an outer force. I had then no real notion of what he was seeking. But as though what he wanted must be there, he afterward borrowed from another the bound volumes. He was like a stalled motor, yet persisting in his thought was a place awaiting the man who could imbue the prose fact of war with the pulsing undercurrent of individual emotion. I began to understand. War was the inflexible ruthlessness of a force that in its totality was but the sum of little atoms. The machine had no feeling, but these atoms must have. Life itself was war.

In the meantime, after sounding the deeps in the impressions recorded, he would do what he could to picture an individual caught in the machine and carried helplessly to his fate. It might be a final erasure in a bullet-torn ditch, or it might be escape to an inglorious corn patch, he did not know. It was actually to the corn patch and the apotheosis of the heroic in "The Veteran" and "The Little Regiment." But this was then as hidden in the future's mysteries as if Henry Fleming had indeed to reach it in the inexorable leading of a destiny. In March of '93 Stephen had written a first draft, unnamed, and this same summer wrote the full manuscript at his brother Edmund's at Lakeview, New Jersey.

In the beginning of June, I made preparations for a summer's painting with Emile Stangé in the Ramapo hills. The making of a set of drawings during the winter was just now rewarded with a check. Lettering a sign to tack upon my door informing Steve that the key was in the place agreed on, I turned my back to its panels and in no time at all the city was behind me.

Many wrong impressions have their birth in incomplete statement. Saying that I wrote a sign for Steve implies that he benefited by it, but that was not the fact. In my haste there was some disconnection, and it was left in its integrity on my table. Three weeks later I found it hiding under a veil of dust, but, freshly cleaned, it was this time tacked on the door, and I hunted up Steve to learn to my comfort that he had not been near the studio but would now be glad to use it before my return in the fall. I told him that everything was all right; he could help himself to the key which was in the little tin can—he knew where.

All right, he had two new stories I could take along, "if you can draw with the bears looking on." I said that there were no bears, only snakes, and they were not interested—I would take the stories. One was "An Ominous Baby," the other a companion tale, "A Great Mistake." Both celebrated the adventures of Tommie. Now, in the fourth chapter of *Maggie* he had done away with Tommie—"the babe, Tommie, died." That was unfortunate, for here he was, grown some two years older and receiving the same home training. His name does not appear in print, but it was on the first manuscript.

Well, Steve was going to his brother's near Paterson. There was no intimation of a certain Henry Fleming, perhaps as yet unnamed, awaiting him. Henry, however, was weighing on his mind and had to be looked after.

I invited Steve to visit our camp. "Can't, CK. Got a lot of work to do. But I'll see you sure when you hit the old pave again." I told him about some big black cedars I was painting in the moonlight. They were like forest sentinels. "I'm calling them 'The Sentinels.' "

He considered only an instant. " 'Sentinels,' CK, just 'Sentinels,' " he said.

Another picture was recalled. I described trees with their roots buried in a wild tangle at the lake's edge, a vast rock projecting its massive hump above the shrubbery. A tremulous enveloping light was being slowly pushed upward by the climbing shadow of the hill behind me, and the woods seemed waiting, the whole forest wrapped in a tender quiet. Time seemed to halt, as with finger on mute lips. The day was past, yet the night hesitated. Then suddenly the miracle happened, and the suspended routine was resumed.

"Something strange about that, Steve. What would you call it?"

"Call it 'The Pause,' CK. I've felt it myself. It's the Great Pause."

He too had sensed it. "The expectant hush of evening, as if something were going to sing a hymn, fell upon the peak and the little man." Steve was himself the little man in "The Mesmeric Mountain."

"Well, so long!" And that was my last sight of him until December.

But that sign was on the door!

In the momentous year of 1888, which saw me on my way to Paris, the grocers of New York sold fruit with the vegetables from stands under their front windows. In 1891 I was puzzled to have to buy fruit at these places from Italians. What were Italians doing in American groceries? But by 1893 the grocers had abdicated, and the Italians reigned at the street corners, enthroned over a blaze of orange, yellow, and red. Then Steve let Tommie loose upon the sidewalks and forthwith he had adventures.

In "A Great Mistake" he bears no name, but in Steve's mind there persisted his image. On one of the pink-lined pad sheets Steve used is written "An Ominous Baby—Tommie's Home Coming." The page reads: "A baby wended along a street. His little tattered dress showed the effects of some recent struggle. It disclosed his small thin shoulder. His blond hair was tousled. His face was still wet with tears, but in his hands he bore with an air of triumph a toy fire engine."

This is evidently a sequel to "An Ominous Baby"; he is taking home the loot acquired in that tale. A further paragraph is all there is to this fragment. "He avoided with care some men who were unloading some boxes from a truck, passed through knots of children playing noisily in front of tenements and went deeper into the slums. He kept his glittering possession concealed. . . ." Breaking off thus, only one stray sentence at the top relates to it: "A wagon rattled dangerously near his tender legs. He scrambled up the curb and went on imperturbably."

It is to be regretted that Crane did not take this Tommie all the way to his home up the five flights of stairs, with his stolen fire engine. We would like to know what took place there. This small vandal was a marauder from force of unnatural deprivation, a socialist created by frustrated rights. But in "A Great Mistake," he is not fortunate. The fruit-vending Italian opened his eyes at the wrong moment for this "babe engaged in a great venture," even though the irony of circumstances had decreed that the booty should be a sour lemon.

So Tommie went back to camp with me in these two manuscripts. Imagine those unique pages exposed to all the vicissitudes of rain and wind and the vagaries of two painters and other tramps in the Ramapo wilds! But the stories did not need pictures. I could not add to perfection. Years later I met Dr. S. Weir Mitchell in the *Century* rooms. Mr. Drake—of blessed memory— was talking pictures with me, but there was a twinkle in the listening author's eye as he said, "You know, I don't approve of illustrations." And after Pyle's fine interpretations! Well, Tommie was of the same mind. I could do nothing with him.

A note came from Steve. "My dear CK. Fortunately Senger wrote me simultaneously and enabled me to get your address,* that I might reply to your postal card. Mr. Barry is still out of town and in his absence it is impossible to get the stories you mention. Have you finished the 'Ominous Baby' story yet? At the present time—during these labor troubles—is the best possible time to dispose of it. I am anxious to receive it from you. Could

* That was a feat. My address was the nearest tree, but two village stores and the Sloatsburg postmaster knew the tree!

you not send it to me shortly? I hope you are having a jolly time in the wilderness."

No date, just "Thursday, 136 W. 15th St." It seems that Steve did have some notion of business, even if he had none of dates. His 1064 Avenue A landlady had but recently removed to this new address, taking Steve with her. His Avenue A environment had furnished a background for *Maggie*, being near the river which held the Island with "its gray ominous building," but it had served its purpose, and his landlady was the genie who lifted him out of it.

The stories were mailed at once. I was as concerned as he for their safety and glad to consign them to Uncle Sam, though even he has holes in his pockets at times. At his brother Edmund's at Lakeview, New Jersey, Stephen was now putting Henry Fleming through the war drill. War had become an obsession; from child war to the big thing, from the thumbnail vignette of battling babes to the big canvas of *The Red Badge*.

Meanwhile bucolic peace pervaded our camp. Louis Senger found there "a remarkably reliable and methodical rain—a steady drip, drip until mildew grew behind our ears and the lake itself looked satiated." Then one happy, sunny day some cows fed rapturously on some of Stangé's canvases, devouring whole pastures. Senger was with us for joyous days in which I did no work at all, to Stangé's disgust. Steve wrote, "These artists—they take such a fiendish interest in their work." He must have meant Stangé. Finally, from a mountaineer's cabin December snows and urgent calls forced me back to the pavements. My record says, "I saw that my door was in its place, but visions of mountain splendor made the door to be an affront. The hallway was dirty and dismal, and moreover, smelly. I looked for my hidden key. I wondered if Steve had happened around of late, for the key was not to be found. Then on the door the square of white card showed a diagonal line or two of script. In the dingy light I peered close to read:

"You are a LIAR and a HORSETHIEF!
The KEY is NOT in the CAN. S."

The deuce! I had not worn these clothes since the last trip to the city in June. Therefore—slowly my hand felt its way into a pocket. That key, which had given me more concern than any of my belongings, had in impish conspiracy with that square of cardboard frustrated all my good intentions toward Stephen, and now unconcernedly yielded to my searching fingers. I withdrew it guiltily and unlocked the door.

This is a veracious account. I was not looking Steve up with any alacrity for a few days. When I did meet with him in January, the incident was closed.

One paper said that "Stephen Crane's *Red Badge of Courage* has had many opinions expressed upon it, but that of a great commander, a man of thought and half a century's experience is the best as well as the most epigrammatic. 'What do I think of it?' said he, bristling. 'I think it is a boy's book about a man's work.' "

That has the sound of a good story and we would like to know who was quoted. That "great commander" who wears the disguise of anonymity may have been a clever invention. However, granting him identity, he, with all his "bristling," missed the point as great specialists are apt to do when it is not a question of exact knowledge. Strictly speaking, the *Red Badge* is not a study of war. It is not an analysis of military strategy. It is not history woven into a novel. It is only a study of human emotion under the *conditions* of war, of reactions in the soul of a boy. It might be called a boy's book about a boy trying to do a man's work. In the Civil War there were thousands of boys. The Union forces under Halleck alone were recruited from Western schoolboys who knew no more of "carry arms" than that it meant to tote a gun. It is well known where the tender youth of the South were, from fourteen and fifteen years of age, as many as could force their way in.

But leaving its psychology to the critics, what was it that sent

43

Crane to war for a new writing theme? Was it the challenge of Zola's *Debacle* coming to him through Acton Davies? I never heard Stephen name either Zola or Davies in the matter, though that counts for nothing one way or the other. His course was straight from the fun of the Sullivan County sketches to the misery of New York's East Side, and from there, excepting for two or three diversions along the New Jersey coast, to the "red rage" of war, "that fierce elation of the terrors of war" where guns "were pitiless in their hatred." The wonder of the book, which for originality of attack and imaginative power of picturing has not been surpassed in our literature, is its grasp of essentials, insight, and brilliantly descriptive phrases by a youth barely twenty-one. There was no predecessor to *The Red Badge*, and it still stands alone.

It was about this time that he dined in Mr. Howells' home. But characteristically he spoke no word that I recall of that dinner, although he was almost daily in my studio. I knew that Garland had sent him to Howells concerning *Maggie*, but there was no hurrah over any entertainment. He may have felt a delicacy about discussing dinners with me just then! However, he was possessed by the war dream, and the hours were voiceless as he rummaged the *Battles and Leaders* in the old bookcase.

The writing of *The Red Badge*, he told Hamlin Garland, was as unaccountable to him as the writing of the later "Lines." He wrote it throughout with the unhesitating speed of one who did not have to contrive incident or think it through at all; it was simply the labor of writing. But he had really lived for months with his Henry Fleming, a shadowy accompaniment of his every move. On the other hand, he said that *The Red Badge* was the product of an utter discouragement, almost of despair, and this I knew to be the fact. "It seems a pity that art should be a child of pain, and yet I think it is," he said.

He was volubly attacked for his "extravagance of adjectives." Pedantry was nervous. Discussing an article accepted by the

Century magazine in 1905, Richard Watson Gilder asked me, "Do you guarantee" certain statements "to be true to fact? You know," he added with a quaintly deprecating humor, "we have pedants. We must always have pedants!" So they nosed out Steve's colorful words and called them names. But Steve's way was to suggest, not to define. He suited words to his need. As to color, it always stood in his mind for a symbol, and so apt was his use of color-words that ever after they would image the thing they defined. It is true that in his later work he made less and less of his peculiar gift, this exuberance of youth. And in proportion as he discarded or let slip his astonishing use of colorful suggestion, by so much he lost his essential individuality. He may have gained in other ways, but the Stephen Crane of the early years became less discernible. It was said that this use of vivid phrasing was a conscious trick, but I know that his writing was as effortless as the flowing of a stream. I saw him too often at work.

No one living in that decade of the 1890's, which included all of the writing life of Stephen Crane, could have been aware that it would afterward be considered of so much moment, not to say colorful. To one, it is the Mauve Decade, to another, the Yellow Nineties, while other shades are given it following whim of definition or fancy. Curiously enough, purple and yellow are known to painters as complementary colors, and if one sees the nineties as violet, he has only to shift his eye to neutral white to find his color change to yellow. Since the process can be reversed, the latest onlooker merely uses the vanished period as a target for jests. "To youth, the recent past is always for disparagement."

The Mid-Victorian called the 1820's rowdy and immoral. They were, but along came the 1890's to twit the Mid-Victorian with moral dishonesty, and it was not very loudly denied. Later, the nineties were painted with at least two colors of the rainbow, and several now faded shades. But at least in the nineties "pessimism had not become a proof of intellect."

There were absurdities. In '96 I had just left the swelling balloon sleeves behind at home only to find them in Athens, so inflated that from behind them one could get no full view of the Stadium area. Crane wrote that they were "like full rigged ships with all sails set." Also, in *The O'Ruddy*, he says of the hoopskirt days, "A woman could have eight legs and nobody to be the wiser." So from an overabundant supply of apparel, we have come to a scant sufficiency—but this is only by the way.

There was developing, in that rainbow decade, a movement against accepted standards everywhere; not a deliberate uprooting but rather a growth forced by the newer life. There always is a newer life, but often it is a youthful spurt which soon subsides into the worn grooves. But sometimes the colt kicks at the harness. It was to be twenty years before painting was to feel the full impact of what had begun to stir among the Impressionists, but writers were already parting with the old ways. At Pont Avon in Brittany, Gauguin amazed as well as amused us. As one of his followers said to me, "It is very *savant*, you know, how he explains his ideas." But we others nonetheless wondered where the wisdom of it came in. Yet we ourselves were more or less consciously at odds with the traditions, and Stephen Crane seemed born with no sense of what tradition might be except to shy at any mention of it:

> *Tradition, thou art for suckling children,*
> *Thou art the enlivening milk for babes;*
> *But no meat for men is in thee,*
> *Then—*
> *But alas, we are all babes.*

To the oft repeated query as to Crane's use of color: "Did he not get it from his studio associates?" my answer is "No." I was the only painter among his early intimates; one or two others he met casually with me. The rest were illustrators or journalists. He had written *Sullivan County Sketches* and *Maggie* before I met him;

then came *The Red Badge* and *The Third Violet,* and there is as much of color in the first as in the last. The painter's color sense is born—so was his. The Impressionism of that day was to him an affectation, and all affectation was dishonesty, uncreative, and thus dead from the start.

5

"Lines": 1894

Sᴛᴇᴘʜᴇɴ never saw the old Thirtieth Street studio again.

Down on West Twenty-second Street was another which John Willard Raught and I had shared in the winter of '91-92. On invitation of its new tenant I left the ancient roost to its gloom and spiders to begin the new year at this number sixty, exchanging the clamor of Broadway for the roar of the elevated on Sixth Avenue. There by the flaring gaslight of an evening of mid-February, I was at work on a drawing when a rap on the door was followed by the entrance of Steve. Between his snow-flecked

48

derby and his tightly buttoned ulster there hovered a sphinx-like smile. He shook the clinging snow from his hat and from the depths of his coat drew some sheets of foolscap and held them hesitatingly.

"What do you think I have been doing, CK?"

When a question is unanswerable one merely waits. Responding to my inquiring gaze, he laid the sheets on my drawing as if to say, "That, just now, is of minor importance." I read the topmost script.

> *There was a man who lived a life of fire*
> . . . .
> *This life glowed*
> *A dire red stain, indelible;*
>
> *Yet, when he was dead*
> *He saw that he had not lived!*

Reading slowly I began to visualize. Sheet after sheet gave bits of color:

> *In cool green hall*
> *There is wealth of golden sand*
> *And pillars of coral red . . .*

Vague forms shaping into pictures:

> *There was a crimson clash of war.*
> *Lands turned black and bare. . . .*

I became conscious of an uneasy waiting—then a swift challenge. "What do you think?"

"I haven't had time to think! I'm seeing pictures."

"What do you mean?"

"Just what I said. They make me see pictures. How did you think of them?"

A finger passed across his forehead, "They came, and I wrote them, that's all."

I read another, which I still have:

> *In Heaven,*
> *Some little blades of grass*
> *Stood before God.*
> *"What did you do?"*
> *All save one*
> *Of the little blades*
> *Began eagerly to relate*
> *The merits of their lives.*
> *This one stayed a small way behind*
> *Ashamed.*
> *Presently God said:*
> *"And what did you do?"*
> *The blade answered: "My Lord,*
> *Memory is bitter to me*
> *For if I did good deeds*
> *I know not of them."*
> *Then God in all His splendor*
> *Arose from His throne.*
> *"Oh, best little blade of grass," He said.* *

Something in it—that hesitant little blade—made me pause. "I *like* that," I said slowly. "I like that a lot." I confessed that their newness of form, their disregard of the usual puzzled me—"but that's their value, after all, Steve. I'm glad they're not Whitman. I thought at first they might be." He laughed.

"That's all right, CK. If you can see them like that it's all I want." And he broke into a little chant:

> *"It takes nine tailors to make one man,*
> *And a ninth of a man is he."*

* As written. Three minor changes in the printed form.

Sung in lilting quaver, this was always an indication of a serene mind. And I am glad to remember that I heard it often. He was not bothered by an intelligently adverse opinion, but the glazed eye of indifference scanning his work gave him a chill. Such an eye from a nearby couch now read one or two of his pages and passed them back.

"I don't know much about poetry," was the dry remark. Steve turned at once and left the room. Feeling his chagrin, I followed him down the stair and at the street door he halted.

"CK!" he burst out, "I know everyone can't like them, but I hate to give a man a chance to hit me in the back of the neck with an ax!"

In *The Third Violet* Steve gives a picture of the antique rookery at 143 East Twenty-third Street, the onetime home of the Art Student's League. "The begrimed building which squatted, slumbering and old" . . . the intricate corridors of which "remained always in a dungeon-like darkness." In this maze were housed various developing ambitions as a hive holds bees. The particular swarm with whom Crane roomed were buzzing in editorial gardens whenever I happened in to see him. The furniture supported the clutter of drawings, ink bottles, tobacco, bread, pipes, unwashed cups, and various garments. Tumbled cots and crippled chairs filled spaces not taken by battered trunks and a stove— probably the "fierce little stove" of a random scribbled line: "A long stove-pipe wandered off in the wrong direction and then turned impulsively toward a hole in the wall." There was "a divan which was secretly a coal box. They made room for the breakfast by cheerfully throwing some drawings from the table to the floor." And not always was there breakfast. That was no trifle.

The men with whom Steve lived used to receive his "lines" as good copy for the comic papers. He told Hamlin Garland that these jeering Indians nearly cracked his ears in their vociferous glee over them. He once pointed to a pinned-up squib on the wall with a graphic profile of himself above it. I yearn now to possess that scrawl which I might have had for the taking. "See what they do to me," he said with a grin. "They think I'm a joke, the Indians! They pin up these slams when I'm out. They make me ill!"

A wren trilled in the garden
Tumultuously,
And the people delighted to listen.
A Jay screamed from the tree-top
and thought he sang
But the people threw things.
Now, beware lest the public
Take you for a Jay.

I once heard a mocking bird
It sang three times and quit.
It was a wise bird
Because it knew when to quit.

I once heard a mocking bird
It was far wiser than you.

Recalled from a slipping memory, these will do as samples. "The mutts yowl like bobcats when I try to write, but I'll get my innings. I'll put 'em in a book, the lobsters. They're a husky lot." The germ of *The Third Violet* was making growth.

Then one day Emile Stangé sat with Steve in my studio. Crane had some of his "lines" with him. As Stangé wrote later: "One by one he handed me the little pages. . . . They had no rhyme nor yet the rhythm of blank verse, most of them exceedingly short, but somehow in every one of them a punch; a thought, suggestion, or pastel of feeling that revealed a new and sometimes startling angle of vision that awakened some subconscious thought of my own." Stangé, being a painter, was also visualizing, "seeing things" if you will, but in his own way. For, said he, "I remember that when I asked the meaning of some of them he smilingly shook his head. If I did not get it, he was not telling me."

Stephen later in the year was in Port Jervis. There was a small volume of Ossian among Senger's books, and I read from it to him and Steve. "Why, that's poetry just like Steve's," said I, watching him from the side, "They scrap and clang and feast to beat the band. Life seemed endless shell-feasts between battles, like Indians."

"CK talks as if he expected the man to write about Port Jervis Sunday-school picnics," was Steve's retort.

He was himself in nature simple, frank, easy. His "Lines" are as frank, but ironic. They flout convention, laugh at pet conceits, cut and thrust at follies, prick under the rib.

> *You say you are holy,*
> *And that*
> *Because I have not seen you sin.*
> *Aye, but there are those*
> *Who see you sin, my friend.*

> *Why do you strive for greatness, Fool?*
> *Go pluck a bough and wear it.*
> *It is as sufficing.*

> *I stood upon a high place,*
> *And saw, below, many devils*
> *Running, leaping,*
> *And carousing in sin.*
> *One looked up, grinning,*
> *And said "Comrade! Brother."*

The more I now read them, the less I can connect them with the engaging personality of their author. They are easily parodied.

53

We may label them as we please, according to our humor or convictions; the best of them remain unique in our literature.

"Mary E. Wilkins, Mark Twain, Sarah Orne Jewett, Hamlin Garland, and George W. Cable are the most strikingly American writers we have today. There is another whom I have great hopes of. His name is Stephen Crane, and he is very young, but he promises splendid things." So said William Dean Howells in that interview of April 15, 1894. And Stephen Crane was to live but six years plus two months from that date.

This opinion was printed the day following an event which to Steve meant the placing of his name among celebrities in literature. When a young painter sees his first exhibited work, he expands in the glow of a realized hope. It is the attainment of a goal. Stephen had reached a goal. This is not saying that the event was of transcendent value to him, or that the names meant anything in particular. He had a marked indifference to reputations. They were inconsequent unless based on commanding performance, work he respected; and if the work he esteemed did not win public applause, so much the worse for a blind public. He was not guided by popular judgments in anything.

There was no flavor of conceit in his attitude. He forced an opinion on no one; he merely stood for his own appraisals, and he could accept those of no others that did not meet his own standards. The glamor of a name never dazzled him for a moment. So when John D. Barry wanted some of his "Lines" read at a gathering of notables, Steve was naturally elated, but it was not because of the notables. It was because Mr. Barry, whom he respected as a critic and valued as a friend, thought enough of his work to want it read. It was the seal of a high approval.

Steve was asked to read the "Lines" himself. But he balked at that. "I won't be dragged by the neck." So, with a fine understanding, Barry himself offered to read them. But Steve was so distrustful of a sympathetic comprehension that he would not even go to listen.

This was in our eyes an event of such magnitude that it drew us four, Fred Lawrence, Louis Senger all the way from Port Jervis, and Button* and myself in their wake to his rooms. We applied all the pressure of combined and separate eloquence to persuade Steve to change his decision and join us. We offered alleged or actual reasons without effect. We urged every appeal to vanity, curiosity, or just plain nerve, but he stuck.

"No one will see you!"

"Say, don't you want to hear Barry give 'em Stephen Crane, the new poet?"

"Come on, Steve, they're lions, we want to hear 'em roar!"

"We won't let 'em eat you!"

"You know what I said, I won't go."

"Aw, but think what you're missing. Lord Fauntleroy's mother is the guest of honor." That was the red rag.

He snorted. "Get the deuce out of here and tell me when you come back."

If the emphasis was hotter, it was Fauntleroy's fault.

As friends of "Mr. Stephen Crane, the poet," we were admitted, but not being in evening dress we remained in the inconspicuous rear. I managed to retain my guest card. It is headed:

UNCUT LEAVES
(Season 1893-94)
LAST READING
SHERRY'S, SATURDAY EVENING, APRIL 14th

The notice in the *Tribune* of April 16, 1894, runs thus:

The small ballroom at Sherry's was filled with a brilliant company on Saturday evening, who were guests of the Uncut Leaves Society at

* Frederick Lawrence, M.D. and Lucius C. Button, M.D. of Rochester, New York.

its last reading of the season. The guest of honor was Mrs. Francis Hodgson Burnett, who read in New York for the first time. She was beautifully dressed in white silk, garnished with mousseline-de-soie, and a corsage bunch of violets. Miss Kate Jordan read an unpublished story, "Conrad Reuter of Second Avenue." Gilbert Parker, of London, read one of his own stories called "The Great Slave Lake." John D. Barry read several unnamed poems from the pen of Stephen Crane, who, according to Mr. Barry, was too modest to read them himself; in fact, the poet made the assertion that he "would rather die than do it." L. J. B. Lincoln, the originator of the Society, occupied the chair.

Those present and still remembered were: Mrs. Edmund Clarence Stedman, Mrs. Richard Henry Stoddard, George Haven Putnam, Mary Mapes Dodge, Mrs. Gustave Frohman.

We were glad to see on our cards, "The reading will be shorter than usual in order that an informal reception may be held during the last part of the evening." We were mainly conscious of the stars because they were in the way. Our own came last, but when finally Mr. Barry announced the reading of work by a "new poet," there were nudges in the obscure rear. Then with much sympathy he read the "Lines" to an audience unaware of the arrival of a new force in American letters. He could have had no more exacting critics than we. At the end we raised the first patter of hands to a polite clamor of applause—this was for Mr. Barry—and continued it vociferously for Steve, making the room resound again. Then we retired to the sidewalk, leaving the reception to the care of Mrs. Burnett. A glowing report to Steve sent him to bed happy, but to convince him took some effort.

The guest card reads with timely quaintness:

Evening dress, Ladies are requested not to wear bonnets.
Beginning at half-past eight.
Carriages at ten forty-five.

But we had not waited for the "carriages."

56

6

Syndicate Work: 1894

I N the new studio in the winter of 1894, there was often a crowd. As I had frequent need of models for drawings I was doing for a never-published Chicago Fair volume, Steve often posed. Jesse L. France, a painter, Fred S. Coburn, a talented, long-legged illustrator, Stangé, and John Raught also took their turns. Steve was interested and gleeful. "Gee! All CK's friends are at the Fair, usin' up the space. Who's that girl on Reevesy's arm? Ain't he the dude!" Reeves, my studio partner, a gentle-mannered watercolorist of ability with a twice-a-week class, who also decorated expensive dinner sets—when he had commissions—was quite the capitalist of the firm. The tramp of footsteps on our stair must have carried clean across the state to my brother's office, for being in need of a rest he soon joined the others, and he also posed.

Life was gayer, now. At the end of February, Steve's *Red Badge* went to the Bacheller Syndicate, and he was asked to write articles for the *New York Press*. We could go regularly to a seventy-five-cent French table d'hôte with red juice in pint bottles. Senger was never certain if this was claret or Burgundy or red ink, but "it all goes" was his inclusive comment. We no longer wallowed in the "Buffalo Mud."

At the end of February there came a driving blizzard, and after a bitter night I found Steve in bed in the old League Building looking haggard and almost ill. All the others were out, getting ferocious appetites but little else. Pulling a manuscript from under his pillow, he tossed it to me and settled back under cover to watch. It was that breadline classic, "The Men in the Storm," which Hamlin Garland had suggested for the Bacheller Syndicate. I wondered if these two real friends knew what it cost Steve in vital force to get that story; exposure in rags to that icy cold, standing in the pelting storm studying the men as they gathered in almost interminable succession—and no sleep until it was written.

I had known that he was going out that night, and so was anxious to see how he had come through, but I hardly expected to find him so exhausted. "Why didn't you put on two or three more undershirts, Steve?"

"How would I know how those poor devils felt if I was warm myself? Nit! Anyway, I didn't have the shirts, you mutt!"

But with a dozen undershirts it would have been the same. My brother writes of another morning: "The day you took me to Crane's room on Twenty-third Street, Steve was in bed although it was near noon—a topsy-turvy place, three cots side by side, bed clothes all awry as if they were never made up. Papers strewed the floor, tables covered with sheets of paper, writings, and cartoons. Crane showed me the manuscript of his *Black Riders*, which I took to your studio. He had had no breakfast, so we had fried smelts in your place—that *was* a breakfast! Then Crane and I took a walk up Sixth Avenue, and on that trip he said that when he first began to write he could hardly think of what to write about—'but now I have enough ideas to keep me busy the next two years.' "

Both being Delta Upsilon men, my brother and Steve met on common ground.

"I recall how Steve once came to your studio dressed as a down-and-out bum, and how he completely fooled you and the janitor."

That could not happen twice! Therefore Stangé's story is of the same morning: "It was a fearful day in March, raining 'cats-and-dogs,' wind in the northeast, cold and miserable. What I was doing out I can't imagine, but anyway I drifted up to the studio to find Crane and another just arrived, both in rags, no overcoats, clothes all holes, toes out of their shoes, no umbrellas (of course not), and soaked to the skin, water dripping in pools about them. I noticed Crane's rather flat chest was shaking every little while with the spasms of a very hollow cough. His blond hair was matted over his eyes. A great wave of pity swept over me; I thought, 'My lord! has it come to this?' Crane, as though sensing my unspoken thought, looked at me and grinned, and you explained that they had been doing the Bowery on some assignment. The other man was an illustrator. I reproved Crane for taking such chances with the cold he had, which he made light of. They were getting the color of tramp life."

They were, and its deepest shadows. Steve had made his own "experiment in misery"; this was the morning after. As this story was first printed, the opening sentence was: "Two men stood regarding a tramp. 'I wonder how he feels,' said one. 'I suppose

59

he is homeless, friendless, and has at the most only a few cents in his pocket. And if this is so, I wonder how he feels.' " Crane is after the experience of the individual again. "The other, being the elder, spoke with an air of authoritative wisdom. 'You can tell nothing of it unless you are in that condition yourself. It is idle to speculate about it from this distance.'

" 'I suppose so,' said the younger man, 'I think I'll try it. Rags and a couple of dimes, and hungry, too. Perhaps I could discover his point of view or something near it.'

" 'Well, you might, said the other.' " And then, "The youth went forth, in a fine swirling rain which was covering the pavements with a bluish luster. . . . Down a side street there were mystic curtains of purple and black on which lamps dully glittered like embroidered flowers." From Twenty-third Street he walked to Chatham Square. Try this two-mile walk if you will on a brisk autumn day, but never, never on a rainy winter night in rags and no umbrella. He found a lodging house at last, but he "felt his liver turn white," and the reason lay in "the strange and unspeakable odors that assailed him like malignant diseases with wings . . . the fumes from a thousand bygone debauches; the expression of a thousand present miseries."

In these excerpts I wish only to reflect the thing that this whole night was to Steve. His cot "was leather covered and cold as melting snow." His breakfast cost three cents—coffee and a roll. Finally, in the City Hall Park, "sanctified by traditions of their class," he sat with another on a bench, from which viewpoint the passers-by expressed to him "his infinite distance from all that he valued . . . and in the background a multitude of buildings were emblematic of a nation forcing its regal head into the clouds, throwing no downward glances; in the sublimity of its aspirations ignoring the wretches who may flounder at its feet."

To all those with whom he trudged the streets there seemed to have come the passive waiting for life to close accounts with balances unpaid. In the lodging house the man who wailed in his sleep expressed to Steve "an utterance of the meaning of the room and its occupants . . . the protest of the wretch who feels the touch of the imperturbable granite wheels and who then cries with an impersonal eloquence, giving voice to the wail of a whole section, a class, a people."

Afterward, Steve wrote that in this story he had tried to express the cowardice that was at the root of the condition of men willing to be "knocked flat and accept the licking." To repeat the line, "a man doesn't stand up straight unless he has some money," but he found here the cowardice of a dryrotted self-respect. So, even in a sketch of sordid actuality like this, he was making his work touch life's deeper provocations, whereas the surface of things sufficed for most of his craft.

His own reaction to his voluntary tatters was "a state of profound dejection." He actually found relief in the company of genuine bums. And he made a discovery. He said that even if he had not altogether absorbed the tramp's outlook, his own had "undergone a considerable alteration."

The other side of the story, "An Experiment in Luxury," appeared in the following Sunday's *Press*, April 29. To test the legend that millionaires have no fun, and the common assurance to the poor that the rich are very unhappy, Steve entered the doors of a friend whose father was one of the miserable rich. Then follows a bit of history, for the New York rich no longer dwell behind the brownstone front. "The house was broad and brown and stolid . . . but the beholder actually wondered why so much money had been spent to obtain a complete negation." Steve wanted to reduce the footman to ashes, "this lackey who, with a glance of his eyes, had called him a name." In his friend's room he "wondered if there had not been some domestic skirmishes to achieve so much beautiful disorder . . . there are some things that when flung down seem to have been flung by an artist. It would require genius to deal with the piled-up dishes in a Cherry Street sink." Steve was absorbed in social phenomena, he thought of the other experience. "There were men equally fine perhaps who were being blackened and mashed in the churning life of the lower places . . . he wondered if incomprehensible justice were the sister of open wrong." But "presently he began to feel that he was a better man than many—he stretched his legs like a man in a garden and he thought that he belonged to the garden . . . he felt valuable. . . . For a time at any rate there was no impossible." But this delightful mood was "dropped like a hat on the stairs" on the way to dinner, for "in the distance shone his enemy the footman." And Steve observed that "the man of millions was in a far land where mechanics and bricklayers go, a land of little universal emotions, and he had been guided to it by the quaint gestures of a kitten's furry paws." But in the face of his wife "there was no sign that life was sometimes a joy . . . in her expression was terrible pride, which, mistaking the form for the real thing, worships itself because of its devotion to the form. . . . It was certain that she never rested in the shade of the trees. . . ." Nor did Steve enjoy the servant who "went to and fro like a slow religious procession." Yet he concludes that "wealth in a certain sense was liberty." Again, the man can "stand up straight."

This story, so beautifully thought out in the details, by a freak of ironic chance, was printed over the page from a four-column story of Coxey's army's peaceful advance on Washington for the adjustment of a dire labor crisis.

The third result of these social studies that took Steve out into the bitterness of that winter of '94, "The Men in the Storm," really precedes the others. As good as those are, this has remained the masterpiece of its kind. It is in Heinemann's 1898 edition of *The Open Boat*—as is "An Experiment in Misery"—and was first printed in *The Arena*, October, 1894, then in *The Philistine* for January, 1897. A note by Hubbard asks, "Can you read the sketch in this issue, 'The Men in the Storm,' and then say that Stephen Crane is not a man of generous sympathies and clear, vivid insight?"

"At about three o'clock of the February afternoon," the story in *The Press* opens, "the blizzard began to swirl great clouds of snow along the streets." This sweeping, pitilessly beating blizzard, the huddling pedestrians, the struggle of the horse cars, the snow-shovelers, the glow of shop windows, is the background to the slouching, jigging stretch of half-frozen, wholly hungry bread-line, that strange procession of men, "like sheep in a winter's gale," awaiting a turn at a midnight loaf and a cup of coffee. Through all the account of the men, their talk and muttering and imprecations, their quaintly grim humors, anxious peerings, and the final crush of overmastering desire "like turbulent water forcing itself through one tiny outlet," runs the night color and a gripping sense of the whirl of the winter's gale. One is glad, with a feeling of grateful sympathy, when these houseless wanderers could at last "go through the little doors into the place that was cheery and warm with light."

A note written to Hamlin Garland in May, 1894 gives this item: "I am plodding along on the *Press* in a quiet and effective way. We now eat with charming regularity at least two times per day; I am content and am writing another novel which is a bird.* Everything is coming along nicely now."

It had taken a year to bring about this pleasanter state of existence. For me also the rocks were less sharp, and fewer in the landscape. The Chicago Fair work was at an end, but I had some money and a lot of proofs, and these were very useful. Twelve months previously, rumors of a new magazine had caused a commotion of talk, words rising like a ferment of bubbles.

"Who's starting it?"

"McClure."

"Who's McClure?"

One of the wise ones said: "Oh, from the *Century*, I think. Ad man or business department or something—gave his idea to them and was turned down, too radical or something. They're old hat,

* *The Third Violet.*

63

you know, anyway. He said it was worth a million to the company. That settled him for a nut to their notion, I guess."

"What *was* the idea?"

"Oh well, you know we've had *Century-Harper's-Scribner's, Harper's-Scribner's-Century, Scribner's-Century-Harper's*, the three-ring show, right along. Then the *Cosmopolitan* jumped in and began to perform. Cheaper, too. Oh yes, a dignified act but more popular. Well, now it's *McClure's*. They think he'll be the clown, but you bet he's got a surprise up his sleeve."

"Yeh! Well, the devil take the hindmost!"

Piped up another, "Say! What're you talkin'? We poor rats need another cheese! But he won't be the hindmost, you'll see!"

"But what *is* the idea?"

"Wait and see—how do I know? I only know it's different, and it will be ten cents."

"Ten cents! What can you get for ten cents?"

That first number of June, 1893, awaited so feverishly, was fifteen cents,* but "What can you get for ten cents?" was answered. It copied no other in makeup. It was what it called itself, a reporter of "the marvelous activities and developments of modern civilization." The world was doing things, McClure was the magazine man of the hour—some achievement!

Then along in June of '94 an article by Hamlin Garland on "Homestead and its Perilous Trades" was published. This was following the line of preparing for the eventualities of modern politics, it must have steel for war as well as for peace, the material for destruction and construction made in one mill, though there was so little that was modern in this that its equivalent had been a matter of centuries.

However, this bringing into literature the business of the times

---

* It became ten cents with the July, 1895 issue. The *Critic* and the *Century* had said that in a cheap magazine it was impossible to print the best literature and art work. McClure's answer was "more good reading than any other magazine —the price will be ten cents—and the publishers will make money." They did.

as McClure did it was new in the magazine world; interviews, science, human documents, nature, politics, everything; and writers made literature of it. But this steel article of Garland's became of vital interest to Steve and me.

It connected with the mining of coal, and "In the Depths of a Coal Mine" was next proposed. "S. S." heard of Steve from Garland, and he heard loudly of me from Steve. Orson Lowell had set the pace in illustration of this sort of thing in his "Homestead" pictures, with a snappy technique which he was to develop beautifully; and I was invited to show my work to the art editor, A. F. Jaccaci. A nervous visit ended happily, and thus began for me one of the greatest friendships of my life. In tribute to a man of genius be it said that August F. Jaccaci was a most sympathetic critic, keen in judgment as he was frank in expression, a virile artist, loyal friend, and an altogether remarkable personality. My enjoyment of his comradeship through years that were too short was restrained only by my awe of brilliant qualities that kept me a student in the presence of a master.

Steve and I were to do the job as soon as we could. The printing was scheduled for August, and now it was May. After a few days the necessity of new studio quarters landed me up at 112 West Fortieth Street, but when the business of removal was over I searched in vain for Stephen. However, if I could not find him I knew where Port Jervis was, so dropping a card to his address I boarded a train with a clear conscience, and in the leisurely haste of the old Erie finally reached the Senger homestead.

From a block away I made out Steve's figure on the porch in a back-tilted chair passing gibes with Louis. "Huh! You irresponsible bird," I thought, "and me all over New York after you! Well, I'll just give you a jolt." They wigwagged with energy. "Here he is!" shouted Steve.

"Yes, I'm here," I answered sadly. "S. S. wants you back in New York." With a bang his chair hit the floor.

"The hell he does! What's up?"

"But not till the job's done, Steve, no hurry. But I'm squared."
"You damned Indian!" he cried, "To scare a man like that!"

Had not Stephen Crane been an artist in words he must have used color with a brush. I was glad to find an agreement from H. E. Dounce in the *New York Sun* in 1917:

I often think how Crane might have painted, but an impecunious youngster painting as he would have painted in the America of his day would certainly have starved or followed Blakelock to an asylum.

But qualified in my mind, for Crane's vision was essentially sane. Now why had I never handed him palette and brushes? There might have developed a new interest. In all our years together it never occurred to me to try either his sense of form or tone. I knew he keenly enjoyed strong color. In the sentence, "The sun threw orange lances over enameled broad leaves," he sees the interplay of light on lustrous surfaces, the stab of sunbeams in the green. And the writer has this advantage, that he flashes a different suggestion to every eye. The painter's color is fixed.

Possibly he was not so sensitive to elusive harmonies, the subtleties of grays, yet his favorite of my studies was the silvery winter note of cows in a barnyard which he used in *The Third Violet*. Notes of moonlight beauty and of shimmering seas in his Cuban sketches, bits from elsewhere that make you hug yourself in sheer delight in the impression, all show lively color perception. *The Philistine* for September, 1895 gives us this:

> *Each small gleam was a voice*
> *—A lantern voice—*
> *In little songs of carmine, violet, green, gold.*
> *A chorus of colors came over the water,*
> *The wondrous leaf—shadows no longer wavered,*

No pines crooned on the hills,
The blue night was elsewhere a silence
When the chorus of colors came over the water,
Little songs of carmine, violet, green, gold.

Here in June of '94—he was twenty-three less five months—sitting at a hotel window in Scranton, he put upon a sheet of foolscap a picture. The manuscript is before me:

The breakers squatted upon the hillsides and in the valley like enormous preying monsters eating of the sunshine, the grass, the green leaves. The smoke and dust from their nostrils had devastated the atmosphere. All that remained of the vegetation looked dark, miserable, half-strangled. Along the summitline of the mountain a few unhappy trees were etched upon the clouds. Overhead stretched a sky of imperial blue, incredibly far away from the somber land.

Is not that a painting? The very genius of the Scranton coal region is there. It suggests a great canvas of a dramatic solemnity. Painters have marveled at the grim impressiveness of the landscape, and John Raught has painted it, but none has pictured it better than Crane in the few words of that paragraph.

Raught met us at the Valley House in Scranton where, he writes, we were "on a little balcony watching the busy street. That afternoon you went through the Oxford mine. In the evening I introduced you to James Young, the Dunmore mines foreman, and he arranged for a trip through the Number Five. After these two inspection trips Crane had his article in his head, and you had your sketches. . . . At my home in Dunmore the last two days Crane finished his story. You had some lamps and in showing one to the family a little oil ran out on the carpet, much to your horror." But, naturally, a carpet is no place for oil.

Early in the morning after the first descent into the mines Steve was writing his first pages. "CK," he said suddenly, "what did those mules' eyes look like down in those caverns?"

Six o'clock! I was just stirring from sleep. "Eh? Mules' eyes? —Um-m. Like lenses?"

"Ye-eh, you hit it. Lenses it is. 'The mules were arranged in solemn rows. They turned their heads toward our lamps. The glare made their eyes shine wondrously like lenses.' All right, all right."

As he read the paragraph the whole scene of the previous morning was recalled as a half-forgotten nightmare: the blackness of the coal tunnels lit by our headlamps; little oil burners smoking into our nostrils; the shifting glitter on the walls of damp and shining coal whose surfaces were broken into an infinity of scintillant angles; the weird effect of figures passing like earth gnomes almost invisible but for flashing eyes and teeth as they grinned at us; the looming and vanishing unreality of it was like the unaccountable progress of a dream. I must think that in the steady glare of electric lights the tunnels are not nearly so impressive. Of those tunnels Steve wrote, "Before us stretched an inscrutable darkness . . . when we came suddenly upon a wide place where the miners were lying in a group. As they upreared to gaze at us, it was like a resurrection. They slowly rose like ghouls, mysterious figures robed in enormous shadows."

I had difficulty with the shifting anatomy of the mule "China" —not "Molly McGuire" as printed (I am using his manuscript) —but several men seized the beast by head, tail, and legs. " 'Whoa! China!' " And then, "in an instant the gloom was filled with luminous smiles. Shining forth all about us were eyes, glittering as with threats." In reality it was quite in the way of being a diverting pastime, happening but once, maybe, in their whole experience. "Upon the roof were vague dancing reflections of red and yellow." And when we emerged, "Before our eyes burst the radiance of the day. We closed our lids before the high splendor of the sun afloat in a sea of spotless blue."

Here at the mines were children who moved Steve profoundly. He regarded the presence of these little "slate pickers" as a crime against nature. Slate was removed from coal in those days. To-day, they sell it, but this is immaterial. I would rather pay for slate than share in the condemning of a child to the breakers. The boys fascinated him. "When they laugh their faces are a wonder and a delight and a terror . . . they are yet at the spanking period. One wonders continually about their mothers, and if there are any school houses." Why was it said that Stephen Crane had no reverence? Because of certain regrettable things he wrote in his "Lines"? But short of the highest sense of the word, his respect and sympathy and warm understanding amounted to something near it for mothers and babes. He ever avoided sentimentality as a plague, yet these little savages brought him to the verge of it. He talked of their assumption of swagger, their exaggerated pro-fanity and outright hoodlumism. But they were children herded like cattle "in a place of infernal noises . . . the crash and thunder of machinery . . . the room shrieks and blares and bellows. Clouds of dust blur the air . . . and down in the midst of it sit these tiny black urchins, breathing this atmosphere until their lungs grow heavy. Poor little lads. . . . They remind one of babes armed with great swords." But their swagger covered both ignorance and timidity. An adult assumes an air of unconcern to hide a sense of lack. Steve later put in five words, "Indifference is a militant thing." Uppishness is the defensive resort of the weak. They were just babes with swords.

The *McClure's* editors thought the end of the article much too caustic of "big business." Crane had etched a picture of Capital and Labor with a sharp needle and bitten the plate deep in a nitric bath. There was a brief description of the miners, Polack, Hungarian, Italian, Irish, and Welsh. To the Celts was given the credit of a prevailing warmhearted cheer and courage, "men who lived perilous lives in a matter-of-fact manly way, who deserved some measure of warm contentment and peace." Following this study of the miners came a contrasting excoriation of "men who make neat livings by fiddling with the market." Relating the tale of a recent accident which had put a party of coal-brokers visiting the mines in peril of their lives, he concluded: "I confess to a dark and sinful glee at the description of their pangs; a delight at for once finding coal-brokers associated in hardship and danger with the coal-miner. It seemed to me a partial and obscure vengeance. And yet this is not to say that they were not all completely virtuous and immaculate coal-brokers! If all men who stand uselessly and for their own extraordinary profit between the miner and the consumer were annually doomed to a certain period of danger and darkness in the mines, they might at last comprehend the misery and bitterness of men who toil for existence at these hopelessly grim tasks." *

But this never saw print. Instead it was made tamely innocuous. When Stephen read his article in type, he grunted and tossed it aside. "The birds didn't want the truth after all. Why the hell did they send me up there then? Do they want the public to think the coal mines gilded ball-rooms with the miners eating ice-cream in boiled shirt-fronts?" To Steve, this soft-pedal of editorial policy was a thing to be smashed with a crowbar.

A small matter would not be mentioned did it not demonstrate the unfailing law of compensation. As *McClure's* was engaged in a war for existence in its days of infancy, our payment was not made in advance. I loaned Steve fifty dollars, and to my purse it never returned. But when four years later Steve gave exactly that amount to an ailing soldier to get him home from Tampa, that debt was vicariously met. If on earth, soldier boy, "hands across the years"! I don't know if you ever sent it back, but I trust you helped someone else. Stephen never hesitated to borrow, but likewise this generosity never hesitated to meet another's need when the means were his.

* Cars of coal were then moved entirely by mules. A miner's pay was three dollars a day in 1894, and that of a laborer a dollar and a quarter.

It was during our brief stay in Scranton that Steve took me to meet a relative,* one of the three doctors of divinity immediately connected with him. I found him to be a charming old gentleman with a most unlooked for hobby. He was deeply interested in butterflies. Steve led him on in his discoursing of butterflies without allowing the interest to lag until at the prime moment he casually mentioned me as an artist.

"Ah, indeed! A painter? Yes? You know, butterflies are most colorful—I have studied them long—beautiful little creatures. But I have never been successful with their coloring—indescribable! And you are an artist? Can you paint butterflies, do you think?"

Steve gleefully nudged me behind while I shifted as best I could. "Of course he can paint butterflies, sir. Can't you, CK? It would be quite a change from coal mines!"

We left the old gentleman, though, well pleased with my admiration of his butterflies, though I could give no assurance of immediate service. Outside, Steve said "CAN you paint butterflies, CK?" And this question was rehearsed gaily in every fresh company.

As I was delivering the final drawings to Jaccaci, that galvanic personality who was "S. S.," who seemed always to have his head in all the rooms at once, stopped me as I was leaving and asked with characteristic abruptness, "Linson, how would you like to go down in seadiver's rig with Crane?"

"I'll go to the North Pole with Steve if you send us, Mr. McClure," I answered. With his quick smile he flashed back, "Maybe we'll do that too!" But neither of those ventures came off. It is just as well!

---

* Reverend Luther W. Peck, D.D.

7

Intimacies: 1894

In the month following our trip to the grim savagery of the Scranton landscape, we wanted to linger in Port Jervis. It was a bit of heaven by contrast. We, or at least I, did linger a few brief days. Stephen lagged after me. He had other matters in his head besides coal mines and labor problems. He was thinking of "the mystic pines swaying . . . as they softly smote branch and branch . . . making talk sibilantly to the wind . . . moving as in some solemn and sorrowful dance." Or of "a brawling, ruffianly little brook swaggering from side to side down a glade, swirling in white leaps over the great dark rocks and shouting challenge to the hillsides." Also, there was the fever of life in the old building on East Twenty-third Street so well known to him to be contrasted to the serenity of the land of pines and brooks equally well known to him. Stephen had favorite words—most writers have— he loved the sense of mystery in nature, and he gave to nature's elements, even to color, a vocal expression. *The Third Violet* was in his dreams, the "novel which is a bird" begun early in the year. And he was putting his amiable tormentors in the book, too, those "Indians" who had lampooned his verse, who pow-powed and clamored in all good humor at each other, but who burned to get their fingers in the world's wool while they consumed cheap tobacco at each other's expense. Even my "cows" were decorating the page which holds that telling picture of a common illusion, "the moon slipped sharply through the little clouds."

Vaguely shaping were other things, too. "Whilomville" was to grow out of Port Jervis; his brother William was to merge from judge to doctor, and the pranks of his nieces and their companions were to blend with his own memories. The tales were all in the future, but the impressions were forming.

In Port Jervis we called together with Senger on a mother and daughter one afternoon, and the talk warmed when it was shown that the processes of a child's mind were interesting him. "A kid, when he wants to do a thing is like an Indian after a scalp, he fights and makes no excuse. If he gets into a scrap and gets a bloody nose, that's glory—until he gets home. Then he is up against Opinion, a Code of Ethics, a Mother. But his Dad is satisfied if he licks the other boy. He may be forced into lace collars and curls, but he doesn't know a fried bean from a turnip about Ethics. If they were smashable he'd get a hammer. They are for grown-ups, anyway. What a kid wants to do he just does, and that's all there is to it. And if we think of conduct all the time we are not sincere. We assume an intellectual attitude and use evasions and we call that good manners. Rank dishonesty! This goes through all one's work. If that is not sincere, it has no value as art. To know truth and side-step it by mental smartness is sheer hypocrisy. Better be sincerely mistaken. In matters of art, we are only responsible for what we see, eh, CK?"

But, while I was aware of the drift of the talk and agreed with his conclusions, I confess to much less interest in the discussion than what I was seeing out of the window, glorious cloud masses piling up, shadows racing sunlit patches over the hills, blues and purples rioting with the sun-gold. So when the hint came that it was time for me to say something, I said, "Certainly! Ethics? Of course!" and thereby proved one of his contentions.

"Fine exercise for debaters—but just look out of that window!" And in the general laughter someone wondered if it were going to rain.

However, editors were waiting. I had to leave Steve to his nieces, who were making good use of him in their way, and were unconsciously valuable to him in his. New York, entirely unaware of the fact, acquired its missing unit of population when I settled to work with the help of an old long-bearded Irishman who made a good miner, though the sooting of his face disturbed him at first. "Ah'll right then! Anythin' so's you lave me face on!" But coal dust would not do for the street. Smothered imprecations broke through the soapsuds, and from the washbowl Duffy came with a blackened towel and a look of battle. "Begorry, it's not much of a face I be havin' left to me at all, luk at me now! The old woman'll be trunnin' me out for a dommed naygur!"

I had looked. The impulse to laugh never consults discretion, but the injured Duffy merely snorted, chucked the towel, and between me and his possible fate was a closed door. But borrowed troubles always exact interest paid in fears to no profit. The next day he told me that Mrs. Duffy only said that so long as her man was paid he could be painted like a rainbow if required, and that was all there was to it. "But man alive, I won't be a naygur on the street, annyhow!"

74

The work was almost completed when Jaccaci, growing restive, dropped in one June day. "Terrible thing about Carnot! You did not know? Assassinated yesterday! And you did not know that? What do you do up here? Are you a hermit that dreams only of his own affairs? But go out! You must go out!" I was just beginning to grow acquainted with the intensely human interest of a nature that concerned itself with my every move for many years.

It was early in August that a note came to me from some point in the landscape of Pike County, Pennsylvania. Steve was at Twin Lakes, in camp with two dozen, more or less, other "bobcats"—he called them—youths and girls and three chaperones. These responsible matrons efficiently supervised everything and everybody, though it is suspicious that they were wanted mainly to serve as cooks.

Steve was happy there as a colt let loose in pasture. The freedom of the woods and the youthful horseplay of the land and water sports were good medicine. Three times daily we fed at a long table, standing like the animals we were. In the orange light of a great campfire we gathered of evenings and perched on low branches and logs, Stephen with his back to a tree picking at a guitar. The scent of a thousand night fragrances, a ghostly whiteness gathering over the lake and creeping along its shores, accompanied the wonder-tones of a summer's night.

"Let's sing that ancient Egyptian ballad, 'The Little Red Hammock under the Trees,' or that old Norse saga, 'Sweet Marie.' "

"Hello, Bill! Want any ice?"

"No, Napoleon!"

"Gid-ap then!"

"I'm a soldier now, Lizette, with a saber at my side."

In the *Pike County Puzzle*'s unique issue appeared the statement that the concert, of which the above was the prelude, "of August 13 was one of the most successful and paralyzing in the history of music. It was really louder than ten ordinary concerts. The

75

enthusiasm of the audience was with difficulty restrained by the police. . . . At the conclusion of the program the first ten rows of orchestra chairs were moved back and Signor Pancako Peti was introduced in his celebrated act with his trained voice . . . as jumping through his hands, running to fetch a thrown ball, standing on its head, etc. Signor Peti broke his voice across his knees, spliced it with a silk handkerchief . . . held it between thumb and finger in plain sight of the audience when presto, it was gone."

This item explains another over the page: "What can I do with my voice? Stephen Crane."

"In the spring, Stephen, you can plough with it, but after corn ripens you will have to seek employment in the blue-stone works. We have seen voices like yours used effectively for cider presses."

If all this seems trivial to the serious reader, let it be remembered that here is not the comrade in literature to Conrad and Ford Hueffer and James, but the boy whose ambitions were as yet either unknown or held in light esteem, and appreciated by only a scant dozen in all the world. Yet he had already written the book which won Conrad's admiration and drew him to Steve when three years later they met in London.

One afternoon it was demonstrated to me that, in spite of a slight appearance, Stephen was no weakling. We were playing baseball. He was behind the bat. I was legging out a home run past third base and somewhat in a hurry. By some inadvertence I had not seen the ball go in ahead of me by a bare second or two, but I found it at the end of Steve's arm. The impact was like hitting the end of a wagon tongue. "Sorry, CK, you're out." Very casual, but effective. I *was* out, for the rest of the game.

The *Pike County Puzzle*, that journalistic curiosity already mentioned, was born, and died, the only member of its family, on August 28, 1894. From captions to ads it looked a conventional twelve-by-fifteen, four-page country paper—seen three feet away. But while "fresh" in the day's slang, its flavor was distinctly gamey: "The Editor wishes it to be expressly understood that he will NOT trade subscriptions for Erie Railway stock. Blue stone or rattlesnakes will be taken in exchange." Each member of us was genially roasted and basted to a rich dark brown. Fashion notes read: "Miss — was attired in black crepe man-o-war-sails with Corinthian columns and lighthouses wreathed across the front. Miss —'s pearl gray sentry-box overskirt was only matched by the Indian corn that grew exuberantly from her majolica ware hat. Miss —'s white satin corsage with green blinds and a brick chimney was well set off by a skirt of ornamental fireplaces finished in hard maple." If Stephen's light tenor was a target, so was his hair: "S. C.—No, it would not be a good plan to make an asparagus bed in your hair. Summer fallow it well and then plant poison ivy and wild cucumbers." Steve and Lou spent one hilarious night in Senger's home editing this unique literature. In an adjoining room I might have slept two hours.

Notwithstanding disappointments and the world's cool hand, Stephen had in this summer many happy days. Does the proverb say, "A prophet hath no honor in his own country"? It adds "nor in his own house," but Steve had no complaint to make of the shades of opinion there. A niece wrote me: "As to his verse, mother said, 'Stephen, I can't make head nor tail of it.' 'Never mind, Cornelia!' he replied, 'You're in lots of good company!' and the inclusive sweep of his hand was wide."

The following is taken in part from an article by Mrs. Edna Crane Sidbury, a daughter of Judge William Howe Crane.*

We children would have remembered Uncle Stephen if he had never written a word, for we never had a more charming playmate. Whole mornings he spent chasing us around, we a band of law breakers, he a "red-headed policeman," to the scandal of the neighbors who did not approve of a young man in his twenties so disporting himself. He was

* From *The Literary Digest International Book Review* for March, 1926. Used by permission. ["My Uncle, Stephen Crane, As I Knew Him," Vol. IV, 248-50.]

so entirely one of us that when someone told me that he had written a book that was making him famous, I had to laugh. Uncle Stephen famous? It was a joke.

So much for a child's valuation of fame.

But while they sported he was taking notes:

"Whilomville was Port Jervis, and many of the expressions we used are to be found in those stories."

Her father was to become Dr. Trescott—"the characterization flattered him," he said. "We were an active, healthy band of savages, keen as briers, father says, out-of-doors all day, and received a boy's training. There are memories of Stephen Crane's own boyhood in those tales. We see him in little Jimmie Trescott when he shot the cow. He himself tried to shoot a cow with a toy gun my father gave him!"

In Port Jervis there was a man who hauled ashes, whose face was eaten by a cancer:

> *We children often met him with his cart as we drove around town with our pony. He was an object of horror to us, for it could truthfully be said of him, "He had no face." One day I mentioned him to my father, and he told me that there the idea of "The Monster" originated.*
>
> *But my uncle did not spend every morning capturing us after a desperate chase and locking us up in a closet under the stairs. There were times when he donned his white flannel "pants" and went out bent upon social activities. We greatly admired the "pants" . . . they started out immaculate and came back badly grass-stained after games of tennis.*
>
> *There were days when he sat at the end of the front porch in a large wicker chair, almost screened from sight by a syringa bush, and wrote. Such a stupid waste of time when he could be playing with us! Our mother gave us strict injunctions to leave him alone, but I am sorry to say that I remember sneaking around by the bow-window and saying:*
>
> *"Ah, Uncle Stevie, come on and play."*

78

"Go away now, Ed, I'm busy."

*Crushed, I went. He never talked to us like that except when he was
writing, or had his white "pants" on. At no other time would we
think of minding him. Any other time he was ready to lay down book
or pipe at our invitation to play. There behind the syringa bush he
was writing "The Third Violet."*

Their dog Chester was a pedigreed English setter. To the
people of Port Jervis, Chester was like one of the children:

*When a pup, father was teaching him to lie down at the command
"Charge!" One of the brothers began to quote:*

"Charge, Chester, Charge!
On, Stanley, on!"

*Thereupon the dog was named Chester, and when he appears in "The
Third Violet," he is called Stanley.*

Young ladies came frequently to play croquet. Beaten by su-
perior forces, the children retreated to the back porch to make
iced fruit juices for the "beloved uncle, so that he could not quite
forget our existence. . . . I think that all the children in the neigh-
borhood who were about my age assisted."

I can see them—it was a ceremonious rite, an act of homage.
"We took turns presenting it. When it was my turn I would wait
until he had played, then go up to him." There was no offering
to the enemy, those

*vague young ladies who were entertaining our playmate and keeping
him from us.*

"Uncle Stevie, here is some lemonade we made for you."

"Thanks," he would say, tossing off the innocuous beverage.

*"How was it?" hopefully asked, for we had worked hard and
thought it delicious.*

"Out of sight!" he always answered, and I left perfectly satisfied.

79

The rest would be waiting around the corner of the house.
"How did he like it?"
"He said it was 'out of sight.'"

Suppose a portrait were put upon canvas by a various group acquainted with the subject, each taking the brush in turn to portray his notions of personal traits. The result would be a joke. But given as many pens to picture the personality in writing, the result becomes a composite of interest. So when I put the pen in the hand of a younger brother of Louis, Walter C. Senger has this to say:

> *He wasn't much older than I, but there was just enough difference in our ages so that his personal habits meant nothing to me. . . . Stephen was a furious loafer, a furious worker, a furious smoker, and a furious arguer. Probably you will remember the time that he was arguing with you other fellows up in Lou's room and, while attempting to light his pipe, stuck his nose into the gas jet, which you boys always kept lighted so that you wouldn't have to bother with matches!*

Well, I believe I have mentioned a certain appetite for matches, but at that time they must have been cheaper than gas. However, the gas was Louis' affair. I would like to be able to recall that particular argument.

Eighteen ninety-four was a full year. Stephen was moved when his landlady took her roomers down to West Fifteenth Street. I think he had little to say about it. I moved myself uptown, crossing his tracks. The mutations of an artist in New York, unless he be a plutocrat owner of an apartment, are subject to the whim of an ever-varying purse and the city's notorious propensity to pull down the comfortable old quarters he happens to occupy. This new studio on West Fortieth was a mile long and a foot wide to the first glance. It finally settled into a space some forty feet long by about twelve wide, fore and aft, with a skylight over a waist narrowed to six feet by the outside hall. One became expert in avoiding fresh canvas when squeezing by easels and other furniture. It was quiet as a village street up there, after the blare of Broadway.

In 1894 here was Steve's second home—if his lodging could be considered his first. Money was still slow in coming his way. In a *Saturday Evening Post* of 1901 Hamlin Garland quoted a note from Steve written sometime in April of '94: "I have not been up to see you because of various strange conditions—notably my toes are coming through one shoe and I haven't been going out into society as much as I might." His prolonged absence from my place was so unusual that one day an impulse took me out to Sixth Avenue to find him. He was in his room, and greeted me with his free welcome, spoke of his work, asked the natural questions. But with eyes trained to see, I made some excuse and left him. In the few minutes it took to bag them, Steve's simple good sense and his feet accommodated a new pair of shoes. It may be that I fell upon a fortunate time, for though at the first he had not been quite himself, he now began a little chant and then turned to finger a little book lying on his table.

"What do you think this is, CK?"

"Why, anyone can see—"

"Don't be sarcastic!" He swung the book around to me. "Look at that!"

Written on the flyleaf was, "To Stephen Crane, a genius. Hamlin Garland." It was a book of Garland's verse. I still can see, in that bare room, the slight but wiry figure that was Stephen Crane straighten and breathe deep with a serene joy. Scanning the page in his hand a moment he laid the book down as a thing worth regardful treatment. It deserved a certain consideration.

If he was happy is it any wonder? Under twenty-four, with two novels written, a book of verse, and the equivalent of another of short tales of exceptional quality, he was amply justified. Here were words which put him on his feet as an artist, gave him assurance in a time of withheld recognition, vindicated his ambition, and set a certain seal upon his future. He could now go forward, biding his time.

"Steve, I hate to eat alone; I came to get your company for a feed." So it was in a gay mood that he now put on his derby, closed his door and went down with me to the street.

In September we dropped apart. Steve was in Port Jervis, and later in Philadelphia with Irving Bacheller, date uncertain. In the previous winter, calls on Raught had always brought the query, "Well, how is Stevie these days? Haven't seen him in weeks." Just so, I saw as little of him now. On paper of The Continental Hotel, no date, came this from Philadelphia:

My dear Linson: I have furnished Mr. Bacheller with your address and some time in the near future he will send for that portrait which you so kindly consented to loan us. He wishes me to express to you our thanks for your charming generosity. Yours as ever, S. C.

In October he was concluding arrangements with Copeland and Day for the printing of *The Black Riders*. By November he had finished *The Third Violet*. Including these, the year had meant the *Press* stories, the "Uncut Leaves," affair, the "Coal Mines" piece, and syndicating *The Red Badge*. If to this time one is impressed with the youth of a writer of fiction so penetratingly alive, one wonders quite as much at his variety of theme, up to *The Red Badge*. Then follows the realism of the syndicate work and the visions of *The Black Riders*, and the brief fragrance of *The Third Violet*, all within four years. Since Hamlin Garland had left New York, Steve asked Mr. Howells to read this last book which he called "my best thing—leaves *Maggie* at the post."

In those days Stephen talked much of the one authority in letters who had first encouraged him. It was Garland who re-

82

deemed the second half of *The Red Badge* for the fifteen dollars due the typist, and who had mailed a first copy of *Maggie* to Howells, and had sent Crane to Howells with a letter followed by a note to B. O. Flower, of *The Arena*. Also he had put Steve in the way of the midnight sketches for the *New York Press*.

There were other enthusiastic, discerning friends, but we intimates were just good fellows who knew things. Willis Fletcher Johnson was an old friend who did much for him. John D. Barry was a valued critic.

He warmed his back at all fires, but in the glow of the praise of Howells and Garland he basked, he expanded, he chanted little songs, and otherwise evidenced a happy elation. I have often wondered if Mr. Howells sensed the deep satisfaction his good opinion gave Steve at that time.

Things began to "come along nicely" in May. He was "getting lots of free advertising," as he wrote to Garland. The critical birds were scratching among the leaves of *Maggie* and the syndicated *Red Badge*. But if the public was blind and deaf, what good would that noise do? "So much of my row with the world has to be silence and endurance that sometimes I wear the appearance of having forgotten my best friends. . . . I have just crawled out of the fifty-third ditch." Someone had kept his *Red Badge* for six months, then he got it away and took it to Bacheller. This was in November '94. Except for the coal mine episode which followed May's optimism, the months had tricked him with the hocus-pocus of empty promises and deferred hope, relieved only by the sympathy of his family and the financial aid of Bacheller: "I am still working for *The Press*."

But now his way became smoother. There were no more ditches. British ears were hearing the twittering of the home critics. The possessors of those ears had their own opinions and expressed them to better listeners. *The Red Badge* blazed up in all its ruddy strength and sent a reflection back across the water so that in its light these home critics ceased scratching and began to chirp so lively a chorus of praise that Steve began to feel that there was something in life after all. The world he cared most about was at last awakened and rubbing its eyes. He had crawled out of his last ditch and been accepted as Somebody. By 1924 *The Red Badge of Courage* was to reach its thirty-third edition, and a year later be placed on a list of five books for boys, but even in this late 1894 it had begun to travel. It was in Appleton's hands in December. There were no more of those ditches.

8

Diversions: 1895

$\mathbb{B}$UT whatever was happening to Stephen from September 1894 until the opening of '95 was unknown to me. I was in London with Cy Warman,* and wandering about Paris with him, while Steve was awaiting the publication in Boston of *The Black Riders*. The public saw the odd little book in April.

When I got back to New York near the beginning of 1895, John Raught shared my quarters. Stephen often wandered in of an early evening to sit on the couch and play Halma with me

---

* He had just written the popular song of the day, "Sweet Marie."

under the gaslight. There was a strategic interest in this simple game which engaged him. With great glee he marshaled his "phalanx" as he termed it, and wedged past me into the winning corner—it was more sport to me to be the loser, he became such a boy over it. His habit of writing in my studio was a thing of the abandoned past. He was busier outside, now. But the one time I recall his taking any note of his labor in writing was once at this time when he held up a sheet with an unusual number of inter-lineations and exclaimed: "It's a real manuscript, eh, CK?"

Raught says, "On his frequent calls he seldom remained long, sometimes leaving a book, a manuscript, or a package. He was not a great talker on these visits. We three had one dinner to-gether. . . . He came in late one dismal afternoon thoroughly tired out. He described to us a strenuous day in Brooklyn in a striker's riot looking for 'copy.' Said he had had an awful day, 'chased and threatened by the strikers, chased and threatened by the police.' With the mental excitement and physical exertion, even in dan-ger of his life, he was 'all in.' Yet he did not even sit down. He nervously paced the floor for a time, then in his usual abrupt way, left."

Then he vanished for months. With characteristic inconse-quence he gave no warning, perhaps he was too busy. But know-ing nothing of his plans, I missed an evening of interest when he called to say, "Good-bye." It was in early January, 1895. "He came in," says Raught, "about six o'clock. I was alone, getting a light supper, for it was glooming and wet, and I asked Crane to share it with me. He seemed pleased to accept, and that hour was the longest talk I ever had with him. When he said 'au revoir' and started for the station I felt sad to see him go—I may have had a presentiment, for that was my last sight of Stephen Crane."

Before Steve returned in May, Raught had left for a two-year stay in France, and their paths grew wide apart. Except that he was somewhere under the sky, I had no slightest inkling of Steve's whereabouts until this note came to me from the far South:

86

Mon ami Linson: Friedweller die schonënberger [sic] je suis dans
New Orleans. Cracked ice dans Nebraska, terra del fuego dans New
Orleans. Table d'hotes sur le balconies just like Spring. A la mode
whiskers on the citizens en masse, merci, of the vintage de 1712.
Frequented I all the time here again l'etoile de Virginitie sur St.
Louis Street. Sic semper tyrannis! Mardi Gras tres grand but it not
does until next Tuesday begin. Spiel! Senger to me one letter wrote
filled with abuse. Ce matin I write un article sur le railways du South
which were all made in hell.

This boarding-house est le terrible Francais, I have learned to ask
for the vinegar at the table, but otherwise I shall perhaps to Heaven
go through starvation.

Yours ever

Crane.

New Orleans
Tuesday. *

No date, nor did I have the wit to note it when received. He
had here his dyspepsia, evidently. And this note must have cost
him more labor than his article on the railways. He had not quite
mastered the vernacular but he was making headway. He had the
easy responsiveness of the artist to his surroundings. He told me
that in Mexico there were certain traits that he sensed like a
native. Ford Hueffer remarked "an antipathetic responsiveness"
and that, too, is possible, for the artist is a creature of contrasts.

Just as abruptly as he had departed, in so far as I was concerned, just so abruptly he returned. One evening I was alone.
A knock at the door brought me face to face with Steve. That
evening was a riot of talk. For once his tongue found freedom.
But it has all gone from me but one tale of a wild midnight of
alarming uncertainties, a pursuit by bandits, and a ride filled
with foreboding until it ended in an almost comic surprise in the
arms of a company of Rurales scouting the hills at dawn.

None can read "Horses—One Dash" as can the few who heard

* February 19, 1895. (Editor's note.)

87

the tale from Steve's lips. I repeat that his luminous choice of words has been called a mere trick of writing, a pose of brilliancy —but here his speech was the same. When he told of his horse's hoofs as "flying leaves in the wind," and the eyes of Jose as "the eyes of fear," he used the similes as realizing their aptness, though they do not appear in the tale as printed.*

It has also been said with more reason that "half his achievement in letters was his astonishing ease of visual description." A very large half! He had an amazing intuition as to the psychology of his situations when psychology was not so much as named among us, with a sure instinct for the logical flow of the tale. Zola, he observed, "hangs one thing to another and his story goes along." Crane had a passion for limpid veracity as against an uncandid polish—he hated sentimentality, a mask, a smirk. And there is his positive genius for compression, getting a paragraph into a sentence; as when he wrote that Colonel Roosevelt "worked for his troopers like a cider press," the competency of an energetic determination getting results by steady pressure is pictured in four words. Conrad summed it up: "a power of vision which he applied to things of earth and our humanity with a penetrating force that seemed to reach within life's appearance and form the very spirit of their truth."

Apart from the time when he brought his "Lines" to me, and when he told me of his Syndicate night prowlings, he seldom mentioned what he was doing. Even when he gave me a whole evening of Mexican diversions, he said nothing of making literature of them. He never advertised himself.

Steve had gone West in January, 1895. He was back in April. A day or so after that engaging evening, he was in my studio. From his pocket he handed me a half dozen or more opals, with the lambent flame of sunsets in their depths. He freely gave me

---

* Mrs. Wm. H. Crane mentioned to me his faculty for an almost verbatim narration preceding any writing. "He told me parts of 'The Open Boat' almost as he wrote it."

88

the choice of the lot. I took a little one that held a rainbow gleam, glowing ruby red with one turn, or azure blue with another. He put a fine water-opal beside it. The next morning I frankly regretted my modest choice. He came in showing a plain want of sleep, which he made up in my back room. But first he told me: "The newspaper Indians gave me a dinner last night, CK.* It's a good thing you came in for a deal yesterday, for the brutes got all my pretty pebbles!" Then in answer to some exclamation of mine: "You might have had the lot but I wasn't sure you wanted 'em." So like him!—and he chanted

> *I had fifteen pebbles in my inside pocket,*
> *Don't you know, I gave you warnin'—*
> *I wint to make a call*
> *On my friends, who took them all,*
> *An' divil a pebble had I in th' mornin'!†*

I tell it as it occurred. In his prodigal generosity he had gotten rid of them, it is immaterial how or where. It is said that he did keep one for his niece, Helen. I hope so. My own tiny bit of fire-glint eloquently recalls the enthusiasm of his return with many tales. If the engineer Charles Gardner, whose gift to Steve these jewels were, is still in the body, he may learn where at least two of them are.

It was about this time that Steve perpetrated a variant of a hoary jest on the editor clan. A brother of Louis Senger was a willing accomplice; therefore this is not legendary. At times, he says, "Between ball games I was supposed to be reading law and

---

* At The Lanthorn Club, April 7, 1895, 126 William Street.
† A song of the time: I had fifteen dollars in my inside pocket,
        Don't you know, I gave you warnin'—
    I wint to make a call
    On my friends in Tammany Hall,
    An' divil a penny had I in th' mornin'!

actually became quite a proficient, if one-fingered, artist on the typewriter. One day, after cautioning me to say nothing to anyone, Crane left a short story with me and asked me to type it and send it to a magazine under my name. I did so. In due season it came back with a little formal expression of regret. Crane seemed vastly delighted. Again warning me to say nothing about it, he sent the same story under his own name to the same magazine, and it was instantly accepted. The sardonic humor of the joke made no impression upon me then, and to this day I do not know just what Crane's motive was. Was he taking a fling at himself by proving to his own satisfaction that his stories, authorship unknown, were considered no better than the other fellow's? Possibly he was looking for a chance to crack some one good and proper!" *

In *The Press* of 1896 there appeared a short sketch, "A Tale of Mere Chance"; a murderer is forced to confess by an obsession of pursuit by "little white tiles . . . blood-stained and impassioned. . . . Always they were shrilly piping their song of my guilt . . . they were flying like birds and pecking at my windows. . . ." Steve was writing "stories and articles about anything under heaven that seemed to possess interest." And to get his material he was everywhere, at all hours, pushed on by an unflagging necessity.

Just before 1896, Stephen was accused of using drugs. Now, in all my association with him in many places and situations, I positively never saw any signs of drugs with him, near him or in him. This is just bare fact. I would nail all tales of this dissipation as mischievous senseless chatter based on nothing more actual than constitutional pallor and nervous habit. His real friends knew. And his own opinion is given that "drug-taking is a habit of fools." Crane was no fool.

Nor was he given to the habitual profanity put to his discredit.

* Letter from Walter Corwin Senger.

Let hair-splitters note the word "habitual." Such speech is the mark of a limited intelligence. His frequent explosions were all aimed at meannesses of some sort, and at such times he might crave to be a Hester Street Paladin who would leave "no teeth any more, right there."

"Legend" is implied flattery because it grows only around personalities. It is invention, not history; fact is ignored to furnish the void with fable. Stephen was called names because he spent nights for observation where the daughters of Madison Avenue went for thrills. If he was seen in localities that made the police earn their pay, he was prying into the inner existence of a phase of humanity that is usually kept away from the view of "decent people." Perhaps if at any time these decent people would see more of it there might grow to be less of it to see! But reading in the old files of 1894 it becomes apparent that this life was broadly open to view anyway, and a writer of Steve's sympathies could scarcely overlook it.

Three or four of us often accompanied him into the Bowery byways, into haunts where we certainly would not have otherwise ventured; once we strayed into the glaring yellow and red of a Chinese theater, where we listened to the screeching of the actors while we gasped in the villainous atmosphere like caught fish. John Raught noted Steve's "quick, nervous movements, his boyish manner, always knowing what he wanted to do and where he was going. No indecisions. His eyes appeared to be looking sharply at something far away. If he ever drank he never was affected as far as I observed. He did not need drinks to keep himself going."

It may not be that all these tales were malicious in intent. But the witless jest carries as far as rancor. An illustrative incident occurred one afternoon in Athens when guests of George Horton were being amused by a young woman's tales of Richard Harding Davis at a "levee" in St. Petersburg. "He was so covered with ribbons one might have taken him for the Czar." Horton and I put the story on ice, but if a harmless blossoming in decorations—supposing Davis had them—could be so used in thoughtless disparagement to make a story, it isn't difficult to see how Stephen Crane's vagaries could be turned into vices. A trace of his own recognition of the fire directed at him remains in his saying, "What is impertinence if said to you, is wit if overheard by others."

But what could be the inspiration of this hostility? Well, it is a proof of the distinction of his achievement that envy should become noisy. An echo was heard only recently to the effect that "only women and hero-worshipers liked him." It would seem that some could never name Stephen Crane without a covert sneer. Even in England he was harried by these "friends." And they were mostly Americans, it seems. For one thing, Steve was heedlessly open to gossip, careless beyond most with his associates. His was not a diplomacy that hides behind an assumption. Conrad found him "all the way through of the same material, incapable of affectation of any kind." And he put forward no "best foot." The sincerity he valued in literature made any pose impossible, and he took no pains even to disguise an ignorance of matters he was supposed to know. It amused him to shock pedantry oftener than once in a while.

But while Steve was not politic as to what is known as a "good impression"—how he appeared to others concerned him little—he possessed that quality of tact which is really kindness of heart. He could pass up the lies, but let flattering parasites beware. In England he bluntly called them "lice," not too caustic a word for men who could feed upon his life and leave a mulch of scandal upon his reputation. One who was a boy with him writes, "He was very kindly toward the younger boys, and when one of them fumbled a baseball or struck out, he never found fault but always had an encouraging word to say." So much for that.

I am not in any measure idealizing Stephen Crane. A credible witness tells me things; very well, I accept the fact. I remember that one breach of decorum does not make a character, for a man is what the sum of his averages show him to be. I assert that when, years afterward, I learned of the tales of dope and dissipation which ran through the channels of gossip at the time, they were an amazement. Their bald absurdity made me laugh. Sneers like these lack even simple intelligence: "He may believe that he is doing a great and noble thing by sitting in drinking places at two in the morning talking to women whose reputation is so unsavory that they were arrested on sight by policemen who do not . . . demand the commission of an offence before their eyes to warrant official action."* But they do not lack venom. Any one of us others could be as justly arraigned for sitting with him at a table. But we were not targets. To continue with the critic: "Mr. Crane perhaps feels that he is a hero in a small way because he fell into company that made it incumbent on him to appear as a witness for the defence in a police court the next morning."

Now what was all this row about? A writer in the July, 1900, *Bookman* contributed this: "One of the most unpleasant episodes which we must chronicle in writing of Stephen Crane's career was that which brought him into antagonism with the New York police. And yet his defence of the unfortunate woman whom he alleged to have been unjustly arrested was marked by a fine chivalry and a passionate defiance of bigoted social convention. It was very characteristic of the man."

With some pains I looked into the ancient files and found that a girl had been arrested on the street and brought into court. Stephen, having previously met her in a casual way while searching for material for his Tenderloin sketches, volunteered, as he had seen the arrest, to witness in her behalf. The girl asserted that the arrest was an affair of spite; that this particular policeman had previously annoyed her and, being repulsed, had threatened future arrest on sight. Also, he seemed to be playing for a record. As seen, Steve held the officer's action to have been unjustifiable.

* From some forty lines in an undated clipping, signed G. C. J.

As told in *The Tribune* of September 17, 1895, a slight complication arose with the police because a letter from Chief Conlin addressed to Steve, having gone astray to another S. Crane, had remained unnoticed for two weeks. The noise of such an apparent flouting of authority added to Stephen's unpleasant prominence in the news, which was of course "all to the good" for the reporters. That seems to be the whole story as regards Stephen.

But a curious sequel, which he never lived to know, was that the particular officer who made the arrest was policeman Becker, not long afterward brought fatally into the toils of the law himself.*

All this blatant calumny, however, stupidly intentional or not, which clattered through New York that summer, was several thousand miles outside my knowledge. This one story I have touched upon because it is related to experience. Certainly, Steve would talk with any. That was his business. He was working the mine of human life and went about with purpose. Other stories which Mr. Beer ably made hash of I am not concerned with. At the time, I knew nothing of them, but they belong to the same breed.

There came on January 5, 1896, one of those infrequent notes from Steve: "Hartwood, N. Y., January 4th, 1896, Dear CK: The lot of truck which I left in your studio would be very acceptable to me just now if you will bundle them up and express them to me C.O.D. I don't doubt but what you will be glad to see them out. There is some "lines" among them which I will be very glad to get; and also my contract with Copeland and Day, and with Appleton & Co. Please ship the whole business to me here at Hartwood. I am sorry to trouble you but I am too poor to come down to New York. Remember me to Jaccaci. Yours as ever, S. C."

The sizable box of papers was fished from under a cot and at once sent to him. In it were some of his most valuable manu-

* Electrocuted for murder.

scripts. Then, in late January, Jaccaci, for some time *Scribner's* art head, sent word that I was to sail with him on the *City of Paris* on February 5, with Athens my ultimate destination. How I jumped! But was I being yanked out of my safe haven to be pitched into the Atlantic? For this steamer's record of mishaps gave me an uneasy minute as I crossed its gangway. However, the ship did no worse than lose a rudder the first day out, and sink a small steamer in Southampton harbor in the darkness of an early morning docking. Bad enough? So it was, and I rejoiced to feel my feet on solid ground. And I was on my way to the New Olympian Games! From the moment of sailing with one of the best of comrades until the final day of medals and fanfare of farewells, it was a time of hectic interest. Foregathering with Greek officials, committees, athletes—the Greeks were splendid sports—meeting democratic Royalties, the hurrah of the events, all this does not belong here except to mention. A line from a recent letter from James B. Connolly, writer of sea tales and winner of the triple jump, recalls it: "Them was the days!—the days when nothing mattered except to be alive. There ain't going to be any more such—not in my life, and not too many men have had better, have they? than when we glimpsed the ruined Parthenon atop the Acropolis through the Stadium Gate. No suh, no mo'! There is no beating YOUTH!"

A great laurel-wreathed round shield hung from the street lamp-posts announcing the "Olympiakoi Agones" to all the world. When to George Horton, then American Consul, I translated this as the Olympian Agonies he said it was about right. Bryan gave me a chill in the sultry streets when news came that he proposed a monetary legerdemain that would do things to Wall Street—it had no sense to me but a doubtful sound; otherwise it was a summer of peace with Horton in Argolis, after the Games. Then an autumn in northern Italy, "days when nothing mattered except to be alive."

But to get back to Stephen. I pause only to note that "when I

95

was in Greece," became a frequent jest at my expense, but that even Steve was not free from the common human trait, and as for Senger—well, I've heard him. When one was in Greece at such a time, it was worth a now-and-then mention! But too repetitious, it can grow tiresome.

9

Greece—and War: 1897

AD Elbert Hubbard stated an accomplished fact in an obituary of Stephen Crane which he printed in the February, 1897, *Philistine*, the world would have been deprived of much great reading. But happily he was wholly mistaken.

It happens not often that a man can read his own obituary. Besides Stephen, I have known but one other, a Southern editor who was once so shot up that, as he said, "I thought I was dead myself"; but having crossed the Atlantic with him in November of the above year, I can assert that he was quite as fully in error about himself as Hubbard was about Crane. The clipping which I saw setting forth the sorrow of the editor's enemies over the fatal

97

finish of their rash work was only equaled in humor by his story of their chagrin when he "came to" and reviled them afresh. But they could not again kill a man whom they had with solemn eulogy in his own newspaper mourned as dead!

If Hubbard had once gibed Steve into resentful estrangement, he made amends now. No doubt the Fra was one of the "fifty per cent of the humorists of the country" to whom Steve referred as using him for a target—and Hubbard here acknowledged it gracefully. "I have gibed Stephen Crane and jeered his work, but beneath all the banter there was only respect, good-will—aye, affection." But the difficulty always is that while vocal jests are understood by the tone, printed jeers are just so much ridicule, and one of Stephen's temper could not see back of them. The pin pricked too often. From this date, however, Hubbard had only good to say, and in 1900 published in his September *Philistine* four and one-half pages of glowing tribute.

A last line from his obituary—"So here's to you, Steve Crane . . . when I die I hope I will face Death as manfully as you did. . . ." Reading this now in the light of his own going, * there shines the light of a hope fulfilled, for he met Death with all that grace of courage he attributed to Stephen.

The shock of this was only eased when I absently turned a page and read: "LATER: Thanks to Providence and a hen-coop Steve Crane was not drowned after all—he swam ashore." Not precisely true to life either, but it was a relief. In his own gladness Hubbard had to make a jest of it.

That was in February. Only two months returned home, lost in work and memories, I found Steve's whereabouts a blank. There was no enlightenment in Hubbard's pages. One evening a year back he had walked from my studio and the world had swallowed him, that was all I knew.

Then, on an evening of early March as I was wondering where to go to dine, there sounded a knock at my door. Actually, I had

* On the *Lusitania*.

98

arrived at that happy peak of fortune where the problem was
not whether I should eat at all, but only where! The question
was answered for me.

It was Stephen. As I had not seen him for months, he had a
riotous welcome. It was a new Stephen, almost, who confronted
me, by contrast a rather dandified Steve. His hair was precisely
brushed, his lip covering was much more than a mere shading,
a well-fitting suit showed a trim, well-set figure. He was now a
bit over twenty-six. Yes, another Stephen.

As he sat on the couch—his old place, but he had forgotten to
sprawl—I contrasted him with the youth of four years before. Life
had become more worthwhile to both of us. He was full of a
forthcoming trip to Greece. I knew all about that feeling. I had
been only a year ahead of him. And *he* would soon be saying
"When I was in . . ."

"Willie Hearst is sending me for the war. What I'll do among
those Dagoes I don't know. What are they like, CK? How did
you chin their lingo?" Why, here was the same Steve, after all.
The excitement of it all was upon him. It was to be actual war,
and his only fear was that it might fizzle out before he could
arrive. I said I hoped not, unless the Greeks won. I wanted them
to win, they deserved to win, they were a little vain, some of them,
but very brave, and real sports. Europe was making a cat's-paw
of them for Turkey, it looked to me. I told him of the shiploads
of Cretans I had seen come to Athens, fled from unspeakable
barbarities, an intolerable situation. The Greeks were like hounds
crazy for the hunt. If only they had competent commanders! All
of that he later corroborated in his dispatches.

Well, it fizzled out, but that was a subsequent affair. Steve was
to have his experience. And he was to learn how Greeks can talk,
as though a dozen tongues are let loose in their mouths at once
and the words like water rippling over stones, smooth running,
and bewilderingly rapid to the stranger ear. This in ordinary talk,
but in *Active Service* he said they "made noise much like a coal-

99

breaker" in a frantic desire for speech long restrained—another memory of former days.

"Jaccaci said that you have a Baedeker he gave you and that I could get it." My little red friend, so full of meat to me, "more interesting than a novel," said Jaccaci once. There went my maps and notes and all! But pass it on, the boy needs it! Only I thought Hearst could have—well, I told him too that as journalist, poet, novelist, Greek scholar, and all-man, he would find in George Horton an American Consul who knew many things besides the price of olive oil. "He may treat you to *Retsinato* if you go with a thirst."

"What's that?"

"What's what? *Retsinato?* Well, I had been in Athens—yes, 'when I was in Greece' you Digger Indian!"—an indication of a perfect understanding—"I had been there a week or so when he asked me to take a bike trip with him. I hired a wheel and we rode out into the country, a morning like a bit of heaven, a violet's breath, and only February; kept going and kept going on a road like a floor 'til I was ravenous for something, anything, to eat. Finally at a little house and under a vine trellis we sat down. A big fat fellow with his legs in unbelievable folds of faded blue balloons thumped a couple of bottles on the table and waddled off and back again with a tray of food. I don't know what it was, just food. There was something that Horton called bread—I took his word for it! Then a garlicky assortment of goat, pilafi, and greens. We didn't leave a scrap of it, and all washed down with the *Retsinato.*"

"What's *Retsinato?*"

"Oh, I thought I said: a brew of 'cough medicine-and-tar,' Horton calls it; but it wasn't bad, really, just their native wine with an interesting accent!"*

* I made no mention of the mastika appetizer. I did not wish to discourage Stephen altogether. But as a starter for the goat and garlic it was fully in keeping —and made the *Retsinato* taste better!

"No thanks!" said Steve emphatically "Not for this Indian! Nearly cashed in down in Florida as it was."

Now why did I not then question him about that? There was the whole story of the *Commodore* to be had for the asking. Newspapers had given it, but here was the man! An incurious habit on my part, a singular reticence on his, and time eating into our dinner hour combined to answer this. And I thought certainly I would see him soon again. He couldn't disappear that night. So we went out into the evening with the gap of missing months to remain unbridged—forever.

But little wonder that he had no stomach for my jest, as he had none for the food he found in Greece. It was the war. In my experience Athens furnished the very best.

We sat together in a restaurant at Fourth Avenue and Twenty-third Street. It was to be our last dinner together. With a reserve characteristic of him when speaking of women, he now told me of her he was to marry, touching so lightly the story of their meeting in Jacksonville that no memory of it remains. She could sail on the same steamer and be married in England. But there were tongues. "The weasels would draw blood anyhow." He hated to leave her alone, but his job was to go on to Greece and come back when the stew was over. "What would you do, CK?"

Just that. It could not last long. Prussian-officered Turks would do the business of Europe's rotten politics, and all he would have to do would be to see the Parthenon and come home and get his wife! It did turn out that way, only instead of New York it was England.*

Just at the next table sat two men talking loudly and not intelligently of Sullivan County. Crane turned an ear to them, grinned, and leaned toward me. "They ought to know better, eh, CK? If they knew it as we do, they couldn't make such brilliant asses of themselves before old inhabitants!"

This led to Port Jervis. Senger was writing now—he later sold

* It is for the biographer to ferret out the fact. Some say Greece.

Scribner's magazine two good railroad stories. Lawrence and Button were M.D.'s—our world was looking up.

It was late when we parted at a street corner, and it was my
final "Good-bye," though had I known! —

I never saw Stephen Crane again. But for certain matters
which are pertinent, this account would end here.

Late in March he was in London on his way to Athens and the
war. If Steve's work in Greece amounted to no more than his
"Death and the Child," it was worth that result. If Hearst did
make a "bad bargain" as Steve alleged—I don't think he did—
he made possible that masterpiece.

They said that he could not report. But I have a page of *The
Journal* of May 11, 1897, which shows how well in a passing account of the day's work on the field he could write unerring
history. The whole situation was in his mind as he wrote, the
insane weakness, or worse, of the Crown Prince, the splendid
valor of the Greek soldiery, the rage of their Commander Smolenski at losing the victory in his grasp because of higher-up cowardice, was it, or politics?

*The Turks went out defeated . . . rejoicing all along the Greek
line . . . then, mind you, just at this time late in the afternoon came
the order to retreat. . . . They say Smolenski wept.*

And at this time the Sultan was dispatching peace commis-
sioners to the Greek government!

He could not report? I say that he found the fact of war so im-
mense that statistics and mere events were ignored so that he
might give full import to what painters call "envelope," the big
movements, springs of action, the human impulses in mass and
individual from commander to private, all accented with bits of
vivid description and telling incident.

The following is a symptom of that prevailing itch to get fingers into Steve's hair. It is from the *New York Tribune* of May 18, 1897:

This is how the Lewiston (Me.) Journal boils down Stephen Crane's war dispatches:

> *I have seen a battle.*
> *I find it is very like what*
> *I wrote up before.*
> *I congratulate myself that*
> *I ever saw a battle.*
> *I am pleased with the sound of war.*
> *I think it is beautiful.*
> *I thought it would be.*
> *I am sure of my nose for battle.*
> *I did not see any war correspondents while*
> *I was watching the battle except*
> *I.*

Newspaper "slams" are familiar gibes of the type of cordial derision carefully framed by little brothers. They are meant to tickle and not to hurt, but this crack has a nasty undercurrent of insinuation, for vulgar vanity was not a vice of Stephen's, though he was touchy at times. If he was found to be "thin-skinned," it was not from conceit. As a violin string occasionally breaks, so did Steve's good humor, but it had to be fretted to shreds first. Every artist should feel that sureness of his own vision which is the vital breath of his art. In esthetics there is no place for the presumption of mere opinion as against the intuition of genius.

Here is a *Cleveland Leader* "tickler":

Just Before The Battle

"Halt!" exclaimed the Turkish commander. "Adjutant, call the roll."

"Rudyard Kipling!"
"Here."
"Stephen Crane!"

"Here."

"Richard Harding Davis!"

"Here."

"All right! Let the word to advance be given."

But to offset it the *New York Tribune* printed the following:

May 20.—Stephen Crane when last seen was calmly rolling a cigarette, a splendid symbolistic phrase on his tongue. He was standing amid an "avalanche of thunder." The downward rush of this vast mass of noise did not overwhelm him, but he was observed to pick up a few chunks and put them in his pocket for future use. He complains that he cannot understand the Turks. . . . A little thing like that ought not to stand in the way. Mr. Crane and the Turks should be introduced to each other, as the acquaintance would be of mutual advantage.

This sort of thing is funny only in its failure to say anything. Had Steve been a bombastic, strutting pretense of accomplishment, his world at home could scarcely have striven harder to put him in the mud. He may not have been a good reporter. I am not saying. But from every contact he made, and everywhere he went, he got something infinitely finer than the finest reporting and put it into literature that endures.

10

The Last

THE United States battleship *Maine* was blown up in the harbor of Havana on February 15, 1898. I was in a train crawling up the Judean hills to Jerusalem when the news of war with Spain was impressed on me as a fact of the day. Near me sat a young Syrian, discussing in New York East Side its possibilities with a neighbor. Their talk was plentifully mixed with Arabic, and I was listening with interest when I met his eye.

"You American? Then you will go?" He evinced a lively inquisitiveness amounting to a brotherly concern in my affairs when

I told him that I was in Palestine on contract, that I would wait to see if I would be needed before upsetting things by leaving at that moment.

"Well, me, I go back right away, I think—and heem, too, maybe." From the comical accent of uncertainty I gathered that neither would see the war. No doubt they derived a real pleasure in conjuring up an enthusiasm for the heroic, seeing themselves a part of a pageant. It was good palaver. The train groaned and puffed up the steeps, the two continued a talk that lapsed more and more into their native speech as they neared the old city. It was as if, fresh from the steamer lying out in Jaffa waters, they were New York Americans, and that, as we all were drawn up into the interior, with the process they sloughed an outer skin of Americanism and at the Jerusalem station became once again Syrians, our quarrel with Spain something afar off and foreign. There were others.

For months I knew little as to how the war was going; then came a letter from my brother, captain of Company D, 71st Regiment Infantry, New York Volunteers. "I met your friend Stephen Crane at Santiago. He's going to Manila, he says. He's a hustler, isn't he?" Later he gave me details. "We were busy unloading at Siboney when there came up the ladder from a small tugboat two war correspondents, one of whom was Crane. He mingled with the men; I noticed how animated and jolly he appeared, the spirit of the fighter in him. When I met him in your studio he seemed of an entirely opposite disposition, rather somber. Our transport was the *Vigilancia*. When I introduced myself to him he immediately inquired for you. He was just full of anticipation of what was before him."

Of course, I knew Steve would be in it. Then it was that I felt my first regret, that I too was not there. And as his going was inevitable, also it was fixed in the determinate counsels of the Backbite tribe that he should be a target for their sport. Steve's allusion to the "mountain of lies" already piling up is given by

Thomas Beer. One of those that came my way was that "he strutted about with fieldglasses like a young Napoleon," when every man of sense was glued to the ground. Now the last thing that Steve knew how to do was to "strut." He had no slightest desire to sample the quality of a Spanish bullet under his skin. He was indeed on his feet while others were hugging the grass—where there was grass—but later recounted this at Port Jervis where Senger repeated it to me, "I was at Santiago to see, and what could I see with my face to the earth? Davis yelled 'Get DOWN! You'll be shot!' Then some fellow said, 'Aw, he's on'y doin' that to show off!' And I dropped!" That caustic voice from the turf was the shot that dropped him. He could stand any chance of bullets but not that.

Bullets were hissing and spitting over the crest of the ridge in such showers as to make observation to be a task for a brave man. No, now, look here, why the deuce should I have stuck up my head, eh? Why? Well, at any rate, I didn't until it seemed a far less thing than most of the men were doing as if they liked it.

There is Steve's word again for it. The fact is that Steve was as far removed from braggadocio as old Chester. And this harks back a year to the Greek war. In one of the profusion of skirmishes in that bizarre affair, Crane was on the firing line when a little dog ran out between the lines. Now Steve would melt at sight of a little brown dog in such a plight as that. Had he not written of such: "Down in the mystic hidden fields of his little dog-soul bloomed flowers of love and fidelity and perfect faith."

"I like collies, fox terriers, and even screw-curled poodles." Well, the soldier-owner implored the foolish animal to return. As it sidetracked here and there, Steve sauntered out to gather it in as though he were on Main Street, Port Jervis. This was ironically heralded in New York as the most important capture on the field of war, but his friends understood.

We have come to the last words. There may be much more written about Stephen Crane, but very little that can come from personal knowledge.

It was impossible at any time for any who knew him to regard him with any degree of indifference. He was loved or disliked with an almost equal warmth. The most human of companions, in our early relation he attracted, intrigued, delighted, and irritated me, and I jarred him more than once, but he held my admiration to the last. Incapable of malice of any sort, he pronounced his dislikes openly, but with the unoffending candor of a boy. What he thought was on the surface. Not being prudent in matters of convention, he often left his circle outrightly amused or drew its fire.

It has been my lasting regret that I never saw him in England. He was pestered enough, but not by his real friends. I was in London in November of '97 when Stephen was at Oxted. In January of '99 when he had returned from Cuba, I was again in Palestine. Then on my return in May, and through the autumn and winter in Paris, I could easily have seen him. What was it that decreed hindrances to the crossing of our ways? On my part, a midnight ignorance of his whereabouts. I supposed him to be in America. On his side, driven by a fever of desire to finish his work, with strength hardly adequate, he let slip every interest beyond the home walls and his work.

Then out of the clear blue came the thunderbolt. From South Kensington under date of September 28, 1900, his wife wrote me:

On April 1st. I was in Paris to meet Helen Crane who was coming from school at Lausanne. My dear husband wired me on that day your address, to go and see you or send my card. Think of it! He had had two horrible hemorrhages then! I left him on March 31st, seemingly quite well and as he would not tell me himself or allow servants to wire me, I knew nothing of his illness until my housekeeper telegraphed without his knowledge on April 2nd. when I hurried back with Miss

Crane by the night boat. And so I never sent you my card. . . . Stephen does not seem lost to me; only gone upon a journey which I will take one day, so that we may be together again. . . .

And on October 18.

I thank you very much for your letter of Oct. 12th . . . your friend-ship for my dear one will help to keep tighter the bonds which his going into the beyond before me cannot alter . . . if I am able I shall stop a day in Paris to see you and your wife . . . to hear you tell of the early days when you lived—on potato salad, was it not? Stephen always made me shudder at the idea of potato salad for breakfast! How I wish you could have seen him as the Squire at Brede Place. I used to call him "The Duke" . . . Stephen was so very happy there. I could not drag him to town or indeed off the place. We had a little park of 100 acres, and Stephen would take his morning ride within the fence, over the turf. It is such a joy to me now to remember that his last years here were so filled with comfort; with comfort brought by work. His life was filled with good. We had the two children of Harold Frederic, and there was always some poor-in-luck or -health chap staying with us . . . and no one, not even himself, felt it to be charity. His character the last year was wonderful! His mind was too wonderful to stay here . . . on this subject I cannot write quite coherently . . . Stephen only got your address from McClure's after I had gone to Paris in April.

All this is far away now! When I had opportunity to go to London, Mrs. Crane had left, and so I never met her, and never learned more of Stephen's life in England. Inevitably the trite "had I but known" crops up when memory would search its cobwebby recesses for the things which once seemed of no moment. Youth is all for the present. Of Stephen Crane, portraits could have been made, incidents and dates recorded, conversations kept—but nothing was of consequence at the time but the passing hour, and that was so full that the future was out of the reckoning. Youth occupies itself with youth, and age is a thousand years away.

To be a pioneer, one must be a seer, with a vision beyond. He must bear the brunt of rough going and the odds inevitable to his place. Genius is not to be analysed, but accepted for what it does; and the best of what Stephen Crane did will not be soon forgotten.

As I last saw him, he is still the boy of twenty-six, full of the adventure ahead. I see a pair of serene blue eyes and a quiet smile, always as in a picture that mellows with the passing of the years. The sound of his voice comes to me, and the quick turn of his body, but it is the smile that lingers.

Index

Index

113

John Anderson: The Pickering Press
Philadelphia